Finding Money, Luck, And Good Fortune Using Astrology

Discovering Your Luck and Wealt'

Joni Patry

FINDING MONEY, LUCK, AND GOOD FORTUNE USING ASTROLOGY
by Joni Patry 2023
2nd Edition

ISBN 978-1-952114-89-2

Published by Madeline Zech

Book cover design by Aleksandar Petrovic – vajsman@gmail.com

Typesetting by Goran Skakic – gskakic@gmail.com

Finding Money, Luck, And Good Fortune Using Astrology

Discovering Your Luck and Wealth

"Anyone can be a millionaire,
but to become a billionaire, you need an astrologer."
J.P. Morgan, founder of Morgan Bank

Joni Patry

I Dedicate this Book

FINDING MONEY, LUCK, AND GOOD FORTUNE USING ASTROLO-GY

To my father and mother
Wilfred Leo Mahler
and
Doris Rita Barreca Mahler

Especially to my mother, for nothing would have made her happier to see this book on her favorite subject Money!

I credit my dear friend, Joe Vitale for the inspiration to truly look at my money issues and how these issues have been part of my spiritual growth.

Table of Contents

"Heaven sends down its good and evil symbols and wise men act accordingly."

Confucius

Foreword

A Mystical Foreword by Dr. Joe Vitale Several years ago I hired a Vedic Astrologer to do a life reading for me. I was skeptical but curious. The reading was fascinating, but I didn't pay too much attention to it until a few months later, when I stumbled across an audio recording of the reading that the astrologer had sent to me.

I listened to it and was amazed that all of her predictions had come true. I've been getting readings from the same Vedic astrologer ever since. Her name is Joni Patry. And she wrote the book you are now holding.

Joni is more than an accurate and expert Vedic astrologer. She is a woman wise beyond her years. I'm often amazed at comments she'll make about life that are shockingly brilliant. For example, Joni reminds people that while Vedic astrology is accurate, you still have free will. When you make choices and decisions, you influence the course of your life and all of those around you. This is not a small comment to take lightly. This is pure wisdom.

Joni's book is like that. It is brimming and brewing with brilliance. I suggest you sit with it, absorb it, and let it help you choose your life path with insight and awareness.

A great adventure awaits you.

Dr. Joe Vitale

Author of *The Attractor Factor* and *Zero Limits*

www.mrfire.com

Chapter 1

Why to use astrology for finding money

"I have studied the matter. You sir, have not".
Sir Isaac Newton - Physicist
(Said in defense of astrology, to skeptic Edmund Halley)

Astrology is the oldest science in the world. Most would exclaim it is not a science but let's face it, it is a study of cycles involving mathematics, in which numbers and vibration are the crux of the Universe. Throughout history, ignorance has kept us from the truth and those who tried to present the truth were imprisoned and even killed. Galileo was condemned for saying the earth was round and it revolved around the Sun, instead of the Sun revolving around us.

This law of the Universe is so simple but at the same time so hard to change in our everyday life. The law of attraction or law of cause and effect simply means, what we think about and say we will attract to us. But the deeper aspect of this is about what we believe. Our belief system is based on our life experience and most everything we have experienced up until this time in our life. Most of our belief systems are formed at an early age from our upbringing and our natural tendencies. Our reactions to our environment are based on all the conditioning of our lives, that involves, our culture, areas we live in, family, and with people we associate. Our culture involves our religion, the laws imposed on us, such as political, societal rituals such as religious holidays. Areas we live in will be composed of a life style, neighbors, schools, climate, and national holidays. Traditions and behaviors of our families, how our parents raised us and our interaction with siblings, birth order and our education have a huge influence in forming our beliefs.

As we grow, we begin to associate with those who we resonate with the best. This means we attract into our lives the individuals that have the same interest and likes. Understanding all of this you begin to realize our belief systems are formed at an early age. The real question is, can it be changed? I believe with a conscious effect, "yes" it can. But it first requires a desire to change, and secondly hard work to understand and see clearly how you are reacting in a way that blocks your ultimate desire. This desire for everyone is to be *happy.*

Most of us believe to be happy means having a lot of money. You hear over and over if only I had the money, my life would be perfect. If only I could win the lottery all my problems would be gone. But for those who have the money and have not gotten the awareness of what makes them happy and complete, they are still in a place of unhappiness.

The Universe is full of abundance and prosperity, but we believe in lack and limitation. We are taught that there is not enough of this prosperity to go around. Once you begin to practice prosperity and truly believe it with every cell of your body you will then resonate with a vibration of prosperity, creating prosperity in your life. Positive thinking teaches you to visualize these things and say affirmations. This cannot work if in reality your beliefs are still focused on your lack. Remember, your outside world is always a reflection of your inside world. It is the evidence of beliefs, thoughts and experience. A real indicator is to listen to what you say, you may be surprised. Do you say often, I can't afford something, if only I had the money to this or that, this indicates your belief that you are limited and cannot have what you desire. For the most part the habits that cause our unhappiness usually cause the lack of money. These habits revolve around our sense of lack and self worth.

When you see others who have what you want there is generally a bit of envy. In this regard many people become resentful of those who have everything money can buy. This brings resentment. Then because we feel we cannot have what others have we begin to cast blame on them, making them bad in some way. We convince ourselves those with money are bad since we believe we can't have it. Convincing ourselves they must waste their money on frivolous things instead of helping the world. This is our projection onto those who have wealth and this attitude is exactly what prevents us from having wealth ourselves, because secretly we convince ourselves money is wrong.

The hippie movement concerned money issues in the 1960's. Love and Peace but living in dirty communes with no money. This was a rebellion against the conservative and what money represented in that era. They hid behind the illusion of love and peace as a front to not conform to society. Different time frames in history are seen through the cycles of the planets indicating the social, economic and emotional reactions of the masses during certain generational periods. My point here is what is going on in a generational level of the collective consciousness will be reflected on an individual conscious level as well.

This rebellious attitude towards money and what it represents in our own lives is what prevents us from attaining money. But like the hippies who lived in the dirty communes we must realize not to rebel against the world or our communities. On some level we feel like a victim of circumstances, always finding blame outside of ourselves for our financial woes. Victims have no power, and blame everyone and everything outside of themselves for their situation in life. In a sense this is rebelling against life because it isn't fair.

As a student at the University of Texas in Austin in the 1970's I remember a small, hippy owned health food store where the hippies hung out, called "Good Eats". It was in an old house with wooden floors that creaked as you walked. I loved the feel, smell and energy there. But not too long after that it expanded, and now it is the huge national company called "Whole Foods". Finally, the hippies of the 60s realized money is not a bad thing. Finally, the hippy consciousness changed! The baby boomers awakened to reality.

Another misunderstanding is the idea that if you have money you are not spiritual. In Christianity there are many sayings referenced in the bible that money is the root of all evil. This is misinterpreted, and in that meaning this confirms our beliefs that the rich are somehow bad. And if you have money you will not get into heaven. And of course if you believe this you will be poor.

Suffering and living a life of renunciation is suppose to get you a ticket to heaven. This is actually a belief in many world cultures and religions. This is the belief particularly in India. For they believe suffering is essential to enlightenment. They believe we must deprive ourselves in many ways, with fasting, and an oath to poverty. All these beliefs were passed down by those in power because this was a way to control the masses and keep them where they are. But even that mentality of those in control was one of lack for they believed there is not enough wealth for everyone.

It is believed that a life of suffering heals the karma, and Saints suffered because they took on the karma of the people healing the world. Once we have gone through a life of suffering we will go to heaven. Heaven is believed to be a place where everything is perfectly beautiful, having everything we want at anytime, there is no suffering, sickness or death and we are with God and love abounds. So we are supposed to believe if we suffer enough we will be rewarded after we die. And all those materialistic wealthy people will get their just rewards, which is hell.

This promotes the victim consciousness. All the saints of our time are depicted as suffering victims. They were either nailed to a cross or stoned to death. In no way were they allowed to have any nice things that this world can offer. It is no wonder this world is in such a mess with financial crises abounding with all these life deprecating philosophies. It is now time that we take back our power realizing this is a world of beauty and prosperity for everyone. It is time to awaken!

Our attitudes concerning money reveal so much about ourselves on a spiritual level. If we can truly understand our issues with money then we will understand our true spiritual growth.

My mother was a very successful real estate agent, and over the years acquired a little dynasty of rental property. I used to call it "her kingdom" because she used to love to visit her properties all the time. She always had problems with her tenants, and the perpetual up keep, pouring money into her properties and the struggles with handy men constantly ripping her off made me not want anything to do with this sort of business. She was in a continual whirlwind of fixing things that were broken. She became so obsessed with the money and problems that she was consumed with losing anything she worked so hard to gain. My mother was truly obsessed with money. She often told me it was the only thing that really mattered in this world. Her obsession became so overwhelming I began to resent anything to do with money. She basically controlled everything I did with the giving or taking away of money. Money felt bad to me and represented suffering.

Everyone who has financial problems has some resentment toward money that is associated with the past. My question is, "Just how spiritual is it to be resentful?" Money issues are tied into our spirituality. It is one thing to understand, the why and what we are resentful about. It is the power of forgiveness that will release this resentfulness and our self-righteousness concerning these deep emotional issues we hang on to. In hanging on to these resentments we keep ourselves locked into the pattern of lack of prosperity on all levels. When you feel resentments of any kind, situations will emerge that validate these negative feelings. My mother has been gone for almost five years and since then I have attracted similar people who continue these same issues.

The feeling that others are controlling us and keeping us in a rut due to financial difficulties is self created. Financial difficulties are the result of our resentments, and lack of self-esteem. This is also why the world is at odds with the financial predicament globally now. We have the opportunity to change our world with this conscious awareness working through our own individual lives and consequently this will shift the awareness globally. Our money issues are our spiritual issues and the tool to understand our spiritual growth. This explains why planet Jupiter ruler of money also rules spirituality.

Resentment and negative beliefs about money can manifest in many ways. Great lessons can be learned by addressing your own money issues. Spiritual growth and prosperity will follow. Our goal should be to find heaven on earth not just the afterlife due to our suffering here.

The great Guru Paramahansa Yogananda said repeatedly we must balance the material and spiritual worlds.

Balancing Your Spiritual and Material Life...

> *"The material and the spiritual are but two parts of one universe and one truth. By overstressing one part or the other, man fails to achieve the balance necessary for harmonious development.... Practice the art of living in this world without losing your inner peace of mind. Follow the path of balance to reach the inner wondrous garden of Self-realization."* Paramahansa Yogananda

We are always looking to a time when we will get there. What if we realized we are there! I believe if we come to a conscious realization that we can have this heaven I just described on Earth. Once you realize this you will be there! It is all about changing all our negative fear driven beliefs. If you can surrender and understand you have been sabotaging yourself with your feelings of resentment towards money or what money represents to you, you will not be denying it from yourself.

Currently this world is going through an economic depression and I believe our beliefs about money are the cause. Almost everyone on this planet has issues with money. The fact that you do not have enough money is a sign that you have money issues. Almost everything you hear on TV, the internet, in conversation, is about money. You cannot escape it. You cannot deny it.

I have come to terms with my mom's beliefs that "there is nothing else that matters in this world but money". From her perspective that is all I see everywhere around me. But looking at this from the proper vantage point involves what money represents because this in essence is what we all came together to learn. Money for most represents power, control, happiness and a life of luxury. They envision this as a bit of heaven.

I do know that my very wealthy clients have a vast array of other problems, usually associated with the fact that they do have so much money. The main problem I see with them is a lack of trust with others. Consequently, they attract those who want their money. This appears as partners who are drawn to them only because they have money, law suits for those who want their money, creating a world of distrust and lack of love. So this is not heaven on earth either. So my experience tells me money does not make you happy.

But if you can realize what money is really a symbol for in your life you can have all you need and also attract those who appreciate you, and not your money.

Money is actually an illusion, it is just paper and actually is a big game we have devised and put into motion. It is in reality just energy and the trick, not being attached to it. This does not mean your non attachment gives you poverty. This simply means money is a good energy that gives the world a sense of prosperity. Money is not to buy things to make you feel superior to others or put you in a place of control of others. It is to empower others. This will create a heaven on earth. And when we understand that to heal our issues with money, which is a positive force and energy for good, we can live a life full of happiness on all levels. This world is in extreme imbalance with the ideas being projected on all levels about money. We came here to learn who and what we really are and this involves our issues about money.

To be detached from the attachments of money we must view life as a big game. We have to choose a career we like and enjoy the game. It is a game because there are rules and it seems to be a competition as to who wins. It involves achievement, with rules and if you don't play by the rules you are out. Astrology is like a game. It is a tool to give you the best advantage playing the game of life. The next chapters give you the rules to play this game to win.

Chapter 2

A Crash Course In Astrology

"The stars in the heavens sing a music if only we had ears to hear."
Mathematician, Pythagoras

This chapter can be used for reference to all the terms used in this book to understand the basics of astrology. Initially, I wanted to write a mainstream book everyone could understand, but as I began I realized this needed to be a basic book including the techniques used with astrology. This basic foundation requires understanding, for astrology is complex. These rules will be discussed further throughout this book.

The system used in this book is Vedic or Indian astrology. This is different from the more commonly used Western astrology. I use this system because I feel it is more precise. The major difference from Western astrology is that all the planets will be almost a full sign backwards in the zodiac. It is actually around 23-24 degrees backwards in the zodiacal signs, a full sign is 30 degrees.

Vedic astrology uses the Sidereal system and Western astrology uses the Tropical system for calculation. The Sidereal system takes into account Precession of the Equinoxes which is the backward movement of the stars or constellations (the signs). This is why the planets are in a different position in the zodiac.

The way that astrology is used and defined is by a chart. The chart is a map outlined by time and space. A chart or horoscope is composed of these four measurements or features, the planets, signs, houses and aspects. These are the same as Western Astrology.

A chart is set up with the birth or beginning of an event. This can be the birth of a person, business, marriage, first trade on the stock market, or even an idea. The chart is set by the day, year, place and time of its inception into this world. Everything has a birth or beginning and an end. The chart can give the events and times that things occur throughout the life of the person or event.

The time of birth sets up the entire chart by the sign that is rising on the Eastern horizon. With the time of birth, place, day and year, the sign and specific degree in this sign is calculated to set the beginning of the chart. The beginning point of a chart is the exact degree of the sign that is rising on the Eastern horizon of our Earth. Once this degree and sign are set for the rising it is called the Ascendant which is the start of the 1st house. The signs will follow in the consecutive natural order around the zodiac. The natural zodiac follows in this order: Aries, Taurus, Gemini, Cancer, Leo, Virgo, Libra, Scorpio, Sagittarius, Capricorn, Aquarius, and Pisces. There is a sign for each house of the chart and the rising sign is what determines what sign will be on each house. If the rising sign is Sagittarius the 1st house begins with Sagittarius, then Capricorn on the 2nd house, Aquarius on the 3rd house continuing through all the 12 signs in their usual consecutive natural order. There are 12 signs assigned to the 12 houses.

The planets are the points of reference in a chart. Once the Ascendant is calculated the planets are placed in each house according to their signs. There are 12 signs, 12 houses and 12 planets. The 12 planets used are the 9 planets used in Vedic astrology; Sun, Moon, Mercury, Venus, Mars, Jupiter, Saturn, Rahu and Ketu, and the 3 outer planets Uranus, Neptune and Pluto.

The next part of the analysis comes with the aspects. The aspects are the degrees between the planets. Certain ranges of degrees are meaningful. There are 360 degrees in the entire zodiac. Each sign and house is 30 degrees. The 12 houses/signs each are 30 degrees, 12 x 30 =360 degree circle of the zodiac. The basic aspects used in this book are 30, 60, 90, 120, and 150 degrees. This means the planets spaced close to these degrees of separation to each other, form an aspect. Aspects connect the planets in specific ways. Some are beneficial and some challenging. The planets (based on their meanings) actually send the energy for positive or negative results. There are benefic planets and malefic planets. The way I advocate to read aspects is simply the distance of the number of signs from each other. For example, if two planets form the aspect of 150 degrees from each other, then it will be 6 signs counting from the 1st planet to the 2nd planet, and 8 signs counting back around to the first planet, always counting forward clockwise. The aspects do have names with Western astrology but they may also be called by the number of houses/signs they are apart from one another. The 150 degree aspect is called a quincunx or a 6/8 relationship. The more you work with this the more it will make simple sense.

It is essential to know what planets rule each sign. The system used in Vedic astrology is composed of the old rulerships. This means beside the Sun and Moon the planets each rule 2 signs. The outer planets Uranus, Neptune, and Pluto do not rule signs. They denote generational trends according to their sign they occupy.

A specific understanding with Vedic astrology is that planets will be stronger or weaker in particular signs. These are very important to know when charting the planets for financial trends. When a planet is in a weak sign (debilitated) it will cause problems. As well as when a planet is powerful and strong (exalted) it will give positive growth. When a planet is in the sign that it rules it is also strong and powerful. These placements will be discussed throughout this book.

The 4 Basic Groups used in Astrology

1) The Planets are the energy sources with specific meanings and rule over certain things and events in the physical world.
2) Each planet is in a sign. The Signs are the personality and strength of the planets.
3) The Houses are the divisions of the time and space of a chart. Each house will govern over a certain area of life.
4) The Aspects are the degrees formed by the distance planets are from each other.

- All these points are used together to understand the meanings of life. But, the main references in this book refer to Financial Astrology.

Planets (Symbols) and Meanings

☉ Sun: CEOs, Presidents, Bosses, Power, Father, Gold

☾ Moon: Public, Fame, Mother, Silver, Water

♂ Mercury: Communications, Media, Advertising, Trade, Sales, Travel

☿ Venus: Luxuries such as Cars, Boats, Airplanes, Opulent wealth

♃ Mars: Real Estate, Engineers, Intelligence, Siblings

♀ Jupiter: Luck, Fortune, Freedom, Money, Teaching, Philanthropy, Travel

♄ Saturn, Land, Cattle, Trusts, Government

♅ Uranus: Change, Electricity, Airplanes, Computers

♆ Neptune; Oil, Water, Oceans, Prescription and Illegal Drugs, Alcohol, Films, Movies, Photography

♇ Pluto: Big business, Monopolies, Mafia, Control and Power

☋ Rahu: Magnifies the planets it aspects, especially a conjunction.

☊ Ketu: Depletes the Planet it Aspects, especially the conjunction, Psychic Intuitive Powers (used in business)

Meanings of the Houses pertaining to Money

1st House: You

2nd House: Money you earn, Salary, Income

3rd House: Travel, Communications, Teaching and Writing, Siblings

4th House: Real estate, Property, Land, Cars, Luxury Items such as Boats and Airplanes, Mother

5th House: Speculation, Stock Market, Sports, Entertainment, Intelligence, Children, Grandfather

6th House: Medical Career, Healing, Restaurants, Food, Service, Employees, Aunts/Uncles

7th House: Marriage, Business Partners, Grandmother

8th House: Inheritance, Partner's Wealth, Insurance, Taxes

9th House: Travel, Teaching, Luck, Fortune, Publishing, Law, Lawyers, Father

10th House: Career, Social Standing, Reputation, Government

11th House: Great Gains, Money Produced from Career, Fulfillment of Desires, Friends 12th House: Charity, Non-Profit Organizations, Places of Retirement, Film, Losses

Signs (Symbols)

♈ Aries

♉ Taurus

♊ Gemini

♋ Cancer

♌ Leo

♍ Virgo

♎ Libra

♏ Scorpio

♐ Sagittarius

♑ Capricorn

♒ Aquarius

♓ Pisces

Signs (Rulership)

Sun rules Leo

Moon rules Cancer

Mercury rules Gemini and Virgo

Venus rules Taurus and Libra

Mars rules Aries and Scorpio

Jupiter rules Sagittarius and Pisces

Saturn rules Capricorn and Aquarius

Strong and Weak Signs for the Planets:

Exaltation is the strongest Sign and Debilitation is the Weakest Sign

Exaltation /Debilitation

Sun - Aries/Libra 10 degrees

Moon - Taurus/Scorpio 3 degrees

Mercury - Virgo/Pisces 15 degrees

Venus - Pisces/Virgo 27 degrees

Mars - Capricorn/Cancer 28 degrees

Jupiter - Cancer/Capricorn 5 degrees

Saturn - Libra/Aries 20 degrees

Aspects

Conjunction: 0 degrees; (1/1) Intensity, activation, big events, depending on the planets involved it may be for good or bad, This brings the 2 energies together and creates an event

Square: 90 degrees; (4/10) hard, difficult, obstacles and setbacks, brings lows

Trine: (5/9) 120 degrees: Brings ease and comfort, and luck, will move a stock upward

Quincunx: 150 degrees; (6/8) Complications, Problems for a stock, may indicate a long low trend

Opposition: 180 degrees: (7/7) Up and down trend, conflict

Vedic Aspects

There are certain aspects in Vedic astrology that are considered full aspects meaning they give 100 percent power so they are the ones to denote. An aspect is considered as it aspects the entire sign, not just a degree orb. Therefore, count the signs as the full aspect.

All Planets full aspect: Conjunction and Opposition

Sun, Moon, Mercury, Venus aspect only: 0 degrees Conjunction (1/1) both planets in same sign, 180 degrees, Opposition (7/7) seven signs from each other.

These full aspects are counted forward in the chart clockwise only.

All planets aspect in conjunction and opposition. Only these planets listed below have their own, additional, special full aspect.

Mars: Forward (4/8) 4 signs and 8 signs

Saturn: Forward (3/10) 3 signs and 10 signs

Jupiter: Forward (5/9) 5 signs and 9 signs

Rau/Ketu: Forward (5/9) 5 signs and 9 signs

- Rahu and Ketu as they aspect another planet can have the effect of Jupiter aspecting a planet for they will expand and inflate things. Particularly if Rahu is in the main houses of money (2, 5, 9, and 11) Rahu in the 2nd and the 11th is especially powerful for wealth.

- When Rahu or Ketu aspect Jupiter, then Jupiter will mutually aspect them with a trine. This in another powerful indication of extremes and multiplies a person's wealth.

The aspects are connectors of the planets and determine the results they will produce in an individual's life.

*A powerful rule in Vedic astrology is that the planets aspect the houses even though there may not be a planet there. When a planet aspects a house that it rules, it will empower the house for what that house is good for. For example, Mars aspects the 2nd house by opposition or its full aspect of 4 or 8, the house has no planets, but is ruled by either Aries or Scorpio, it will empower that house. The 2nd house will then be empowered by Mars. This will give the good effects of what the house rules in life. The 2nd house rules money, so it will be extra powerful to produce money in the person's life. This holds true even if the planet is a malefic such as Sun, Mars, or Saturn.

Nakshatras

Vedic astrology uses the 27 nakshatras. They are used like the signs. They are 13 degrees and 20 minutes divisions of the zodiac. The signs are 30 degree portions. They are very specific and are actually the bases of Vedic astrology, because the entire predictive system, called the Dashas, is based on the placement of the Moon's nakshatra. They determine the entire life cycle in a person's life. Used here, there are very specific nakshatras that pertain to wealth and money. The fixed stars in these portions of the sky give qualities of the powerful influences the nakshatras can exert on to a chart or individual. Certain nakshatras will be referenced throughout this book.

Transits

Once a chart has been calculated it is a map of where the planets are in a certain time and place. The moving planets in the sky are called the transiting planets. To chart the future trends in a person's life or of any event involves the transiting planets. The transiting planets are placed against the planets in a birth chart (natal) to make predictions for the future. To know where and when a transiting planet will move through a particular house in a birth chart will indicate the events and experiences the individual will experience. The signs they are transiting will determine the strength or weakness in effects. The aspects of the transiting planets to the birth planets in a chart will be the timing of events in a person's life. Or, if the chart is of a business it can predict growth and expansion or a decline in business. We can chart the future aspects as to the day and time that hit a personal planet in a birth chart through their aspects.

	Nakshatras		**Degrees**
1	Ashwini	"the horse woman"	00:00 ♈ to 13:20 ♈
2	Bharani	"the bearer - of new life"	13:20 ♈ to 26:40 ♈
3	Krittika	"the one who cuts"	26:40 ♈ to 10:00 ♉
4	Rohini	"the red one"	10:00 ♉ to 23:20 ♉
5	Mrigashira	"head of a deer"	23:20 ♉ to 06:40 ♊
6	Ardra	"the moist one"	06:40 ♊ to 20:00 ♊
7	Purnavasu	"return of the light"	20:00 ♊ to 03:20 ♋
8	Pushya	"to nourish"	03:20 ♋ to 16:40 ♋
9	Ashlesha	"the embracer"	16:40 ♋ to 30:00 ♋
10	Magha	"the great one"	00:00 ♌ to 13:20 ♌
11	Purva Phalguni	"the former reddish one"	13:20 ♌ to 26:40 ♌
12	Uttara Phalguni	"the later reddish one"	26:40 ♌ to 10:00 ♍
13	Hasta	"the hand"	10:00 ♍ to 23:20 ♍
14	Chitra	"the bright one"	23:20 ♍ to 06:40 ♎
15	Swati	"the sword or independence"	06:40 ♎ to 20:00 ♎
16	Vishakha	"the forked shaped"	20:00 ♎ to 03:20 ♏
17	Anuradha	"the discipline of the divine spark"	03:20 ♏ to 16:40 ♏
18	Jyeshta	"the eldest"	16:40 ♏ to 00:00 ♐
19	Mula	"the root"	00:00 ♐ to 13:20 ♐
20	Purva Ashadha	"early victory"	13:20 ♐ to 26:40 ♐
21	Uttara Ashadha	"latter victory"	26:40 ♐ to 10:00 ♑
22	Shravana	"the ear"	10:00 ♑ to 23:20 ♑
23	Dhanishta	"the richest one"	23:20 ♑ to 06:40 ♒
24	Shatabishak	"the hundred healers"	06:40 ♒ to 20:00 ♒
25	P: Bhadrapada	"the former happy feet"	20:00 ♒ to 03:20 ♓
26	U: Bhadrapada	"the latter happy feet"	03:20 ♓ to 16:40 ♓
27	Revati	"the wealthiest one"	16:40 ♓ to 30:00 ♓

Chapter 3

How to Predict World Events with Astrology

"The celestial bodies are the cause of all that takes place in the sublunar world."

St. Thomas Aquinas

Each year I study the patterns of the planets to get a feel for the next year. Once I have studied and understood the patterns and cycles that will be forming each month of the year, I then plug these patterns into every client's chart I analyze.

Each year definitely has unique patterns with different distinctive relationships. The exact combinations will never be repeated, but there are definite similarities. It is very interesting to know what trends will come out of the year and to know when and how things will unfold.

It is interesting to see the global events mirror the dispositions of the planet's positions. We have to wonder if the entire global climate is instigated by the positions of the planets. Within these parameters of the global events, it is then brought down to each individual and their individual planetary patterns. These are the effects on the masses, and how it affects each individual on the planet. As above so below! Everything outside of each of us is a reflection of what is going on inside each of us. If we are to understand the planetary symbols and physics of these planets and how they relate to us, we will have the answers for all of mankind.

Through astrology we can identify what will be the most powerful experiences to promote our growth as humankind, the masses and how this will be experienced through each individual. We are individually affected by the experience of the masses and we grow together as humankind. Through astrology messages are seen through the patterns in the heavenly sky and reveal to us lessons and trends globally and personally.

To get a feel for each year the most significant planets to analyze are Jupiter and Saturn. These two planets are called the social planets, mainly because they do indicate the social climate of the people of planet Earth. Jupiter is in a sign for one year and travels through the entire 12 signs of the zodiac in 12 years. Saturn stays in a sign for 2 !4 years, and takes 30 years to travel through the entire zodiac. The aspects between these 2 planets give an amazing amount of information about the year in question. The signs they are in are extremely important too. This can definitely shape the year in terms of the financial markets. When these planets are in signs where they are strong, the economy is prosperous. The aspect between these 2 planets is imperative to understand the financial climate of the year. Both Jupiter and Saturn, the signs they reside and the aspects they form to each other, are the most important indicators for the year's financial trends.

Signs that Jupiter prospers or declines in energy:

Strongest: Cancer,
Very Strong; Pisces, Sagittarius
Strong: Scorpio, Leo
Weakest: Capricorn
Very Weak: Gemini, Libra, Virgo, Taurus
Weak: Aquarius

Signs Saturn prospers or declines in energy:

Strongest: Libra
Very strong: Capricorn and Aquarius
Strong: Taurus, Gemini, Virgo
Weakest: Aries Very
Weak: Leo, Scorpio
Weak: Sagittarius, Cancer, Pisces

Aspects

Aspects are the degrees between the planets, but counting the number of signs they are from each other is a much easier way to identify and understand the aspects. The numerical significance of these aspect numbers becomes meaningful. The first number is the number of signs counted from the 1st planet to the 2nd planet. The second number is the number of signs counted, continuing forward back to the 1st planet. Within the Vedic chart you are counting clockwise. There are positive combinations and negative combinations.

Aspects between Jupiter and Saturn

1/1 (Conjunction): Both Jupiter and Saturn are in the same sign and house. Intense, big events, turning points, Jupiter and Saturn will form a conjunction every 20 years and is noted for extraordinary events concerning political leaders and big sways in the financial markets.

2/12 (Semi Sextile) Both Jupiter and Saturn are in a sign right next to each other. This is not harmonious; there are unresolved matters that never get solved. There are some losses that are necessary to get a resolution to matters.

3/11 (sextile) Events flow smoothly, the economy improves. This is a time for opportunities particularly in the job markets, new growth takes place.

4/10 (Square) Growth through hard work and effort, there will be big events that create massive growth, many changes politically that will expand the economy, more opportunities.

5/9 (Trine) Ease and comfort create a great economic flow. This is the best aspect between Saturn and Jupiter. Much prosperity, the economy flourishes

6/8 (Quincunx) This is the worst aspect between Jupiter and Saturn. This means everything is out of harmony. Extreme overextended economy creates overload and imbalance and must now be fixed. Lowest point in the economy.

7/7 (Opposition) There is an imbalance that must be worked out. There are opposing forces that must be balanced. It will involve compromise.

In 2008-2009 Jupiter was in Capricorn the weakest sign for Jupiter indicating a very difficult year economically. And Saturn was in Leo a sign that is very bad for Saturn for it cannot bring people together to work things out. The aspect between Jupiter and Saturn was the 6/8 (Quincunx) meaning the world and economy was very difficult with no end in sight. This was the year the economy hit a low and was compared to the years of the Great Depression. The banks and the car industry needed the government to lend them huge amounts of money so they would not fail. Many lost their jobs and homes. This was definitely predicted by the placements of both Jupiter and Saturn at this time.

The Lunar Nodes: Rahu/ Ketu and Eclipses for World Predictions

There is an absolute secret to the astrological cycles that will apply across the board in any life event using an astrological chart. This means if you are looking at the chart of a person, business, stock, marriage, or "anything". This principal will absolutely apply in every case.

The first principal involves the lunar nodes for they dictate every cycle that occurs in our life. Their cycles are tied into the cycles of Saturn and Jupiter determining the specific yearly trends. When you calculate the transits of these planets to the natal planets in an individual's chart you will see clearly any life development. They will be forming different combinations throughout life, but these combinations are what predict our life events as a whole.

First, the lunar nodes are what cause the web of life. They are our karma as a soul and their cycles determine our earthly cycle. The Sun is our body and the Moon is our mind. The nodes become strongest around the time of eclipses, when the Sun and Moon line up with the nodes. Many myths and stories abound concerning this fact.

In Vedic astrology Rahu is the north node of the Moon and Ketu is the south node of the Moon. Rahu is the ascending node of the Moon which means it is the place on the ecliptic (the apparent path of the Sun around the Earth) where the Moon hits the ecliptic moving upward. And Ketu is the place on the ecliptic where the Moon crosses the ecliptic moving downward. These points are exactly opposite each other therefore; their zodiacal degrees will be precisely the same degree but exactly opposite signs in the zodiac.

This is symbolic of our entrapment into this Earthly plane, or how our mind traps us into this world, but our understanding of the spirit liberates us. For Rahu represents the physical and the mind and Ketu represents the spirit and the spiritual.

In ancient Vedic myth there was a line-up of the planets to receive the nectar of Amrita which when drank will give immortality. But suddenly a serpent slithers between the Sun and the Moon to drink this Amrita. The Sun and the Moon called out to Lord Shiva (the king of the gods) and he threw a disc which sliced the creature in half. But, unfortunately the serpent had already swallowed the nectar. Therefore; we have the serpent's head (Rahu) and the serpent's tail (Ketu). Some call it the dragon's head and the dragon's tail.

You can see why from this myth Rahu is the head therefore; concerns the mind without the heart and soul, and Ketu is the tail which is the body without the head, denoting the heart and soul. Rahu in astrology rules the materialistic Earthly world and will concern itself with the mind and all of its obsessions and attachments. Conversely, Ketu rules our intuition or our gut knowing of things without the mind. Rahu is our entrance into this world with all our karma, worldly desires and attachments, while Ketu is our release from this world through our understanding of our spiritual purpose which involves the release of our materialistic attachments. You could say Rahu is birth into this world and Ketu is the death of this world.

With this specific understanding of these two most important features in a chart, you will come to realize they direct the cycles in our lives. The Nodes of the Moon (Rahu and Ketu) change signs every 18 months (1 14 year), and take 18 14 years to transit through the entire 12 zodiacal signs. This means it takes 18 14 years in your life for Rahu and Ketu to return to the same place they were when you were born. Every 18 14 years we have a big change in life or a new beginning. It is no surprise that we all graduate from high school around this time and leave our homes. But since Rahu and Ketu are points that exactly oppose each other this means that around each 9 years (half of the cycle of Rahu and Ketu) the transit of Rahu will conjoin the place where Ketu was at birth, and transiting Ketu will conjoin the place where Rahu was at birth.

As these harbingers of fate and destiny transit through your chart, they depict the major cycles of change throughout life. Each sign they transit through each 18 months will change your life according to where your natal planets are placed. And around each 18 years you have a life change. These occur around age 18, 36, 54, 72 and 90 years of age.

The next specific points to be tracked in a birth chart are the powerful planets Jupiter and Saturn. These are called the social planets because they depict the social climate of the world as they revolve through the 12 zodiacal signs.

These two planets are diametrically opposite in there symbolic meanings. Jupiter symbolizes expansion, growth, wealth, and excess, while Saturn symbolizes restriction, endings, poverty, structure and discipline.

Their cycles through the zodiac are very explicit and easy to track. Jupiter will take one year to travel through one zodiacal sign therefore; it takes 12 years to transit the entire zodiac of 12 signs. Saturn takes 2 14 years to travel through one sign of the zodiac therefore; it takes about 30 years to travel through the 12 signs of the zodiac.

Here is the Big Secret concerning all astrological cycles: the cycles of the Lunar nodes (Rahu and Ketu) combined with the cycles of Jupiter and Saturn determine the cycles of our life.

This means there is a pattern always forming between these heavenly points in the sky and their relationship to these same points in our chart that determine our destiny. I am referring to the transits in the sky and their relationship to each other, and the relationship of these same planets in a birth chart.

Rahu and Ketu combined with Jupiter and Saturn must be observed in the sky as they transit through the signs and their relationships to each other. There are certain planetary arrangements that produce specific meanings and consequently events. These arrangements are called aspects. They are the distances that each of these planets form from one another.

Always bear in mind that Rahu and Ketu are always exactly opposite each other, which means they are in opposition. They move with this opposition always lined up. Remember, they are not actually planets but points in the sky where the Moon crosses the ecliptic, but we will still refer to them as planets. The Nodes of the Moon have a very different orbit than the actual planets because they travel backwards in the zodiac instead of the forward motion of the planets. There are times when the movements of the planets do appear to go backwards which is called retrograde motion.

It is the aspects that these four points (Rahu/Ketu and Jupiter/Saturn) form that depict our ups and downs in our life. The combinations of these transiting points in the heavens are what determine the events that occur on our planet Earth. But with respect to each individual human being, it is the natal relationships of these four points in their birth chart that sets up their life's path.

It is the aspects, formed by these four planets transiting in the heavens, applied in relationship to our birth charts that will determine our life's experiences. That is basically the secret to astrology. This may sound easy, but there are so many combinations that it will seem very complex. There are of course many other variables involved concerning the other planets in a chart. But, remember to first concentrate on the features of these four planets combined and apply them to these same natal four planets in a birth chart and you will see the grand cycles of life unfold.

The most amazing thing you will find with this practice is you can find the specific times that you are more fortunate and times when you need to lay low. These fortunate times are used in your favor to make forward movement, and the other times are when <u>not</u> to move forward. These principals can be used in lottery wins, gambling, and applied through the stock market. If you can positively predict the rise and fall of a cycle you can produce productivity in your life

Like the tones in music there are some aspects in astrology that are in complete harmony and some that are off key which is not in harmony. The aspects that are the most harmonious are the trine and then the sextile, which are 120 degrees and 60 degrees, or 5/ 9 and 3/11 signs apart. The trine is definitely the most harmonious. But the aspect that is the most inharmonic is the quincunx and the square, the quincunx is the most difficult. The quincunx is 150 degrees and the square is 90 degrees, or 6 /8 signs apart and 4/10 signs apart.

Within a natal birth chart these four planet's placements will indicate if life is easy or hard. The trines and sextiles will give ease and comfort in life and the quincunxes and squares will give challenges. When you have a combination of both the trines with the sextiles in the chart this will be the most powerful for successful events in a life.

The planets that dictate social and generational change globally are the three outer planets, Uranus, Neptune, and Pluto. They specifically influence the mass consciousness, and are transpersonal. The forming aspects between these 3 outer planets, the 2 social planets, Jupiter and Saturn within the confines of Rahu and Ketu reveal the mass consciousness and global developments. This reveals the political, financial, and societal climate in the world, year after year by understanding the planetary patterns in the heavens. In terms of the financial climate, the understanding of these outer planets from year to year determines many ups and downs in the markets. The slower a planet moves the more of an impact it will have on global affairs. The three outer planets actually determine specific eras with their combinations or patterns. It is their relationships to each other that predict the movements and eras in history.

Also, when a planet turns retrograde it slows and appears to stop which makes it significant. I am referring to the inner personal planets Mercury, Venus and Mars. Their retrograde cycles within the grand cycles of the slower moving planets are indicative of the emotions of the masses, therefore affecting the stock market.

It is important to understand the symbology of the outer planets to apply their meanings to the global markets and predictions for all global affairs. Their formation to one another are always an entirely different pattern, like each finger print is unique and one of a kind. But there are definite similarities with the patterns of the planets in the past. Therefore, we can draw from the events that occurred before to help us understand certain planetary configurations.

Another interesting effect is the planet's patterns, that determine an era in history, will be the same patterns in the individual's charts that are born during those times. This shapes the personalities of the individuals born during specific times in history. So, the outer planets and their formations during certain times are what make certain generations different, for these formations will be a part of their individual charts.

The outer planets are what form the social climate of the times and form the generations of those times, so I call the outer planets "generational". They influence the entire generation of that time.

When these outer planets were discovered it is important to understand what they represented came into consciousness during the time of their discovery. Only with hindsight can we see exactly what these planets brought into awareness.

♅ **Uranus:** Uranus was discovered in 1781. This was around the onset of the industrial revolution. Inventions were discovered to make work and trade possible on a global scale. The use of electricity and inventions like the cotton gin were beginning. All this opened the world to mass communications.

Rules: Change, eccentricity, rebellion, erratic behavior, sudden and unexpected happenings, shock, earthquakes, lightning, electricity, computers, inventions, airplanes, astrology.

♆ **Neptune:** Neptune was discovered around 1846. At this time photography was beginning, symbolic of Neptune's creation of illusions that seem real, as in photos or films. This was the onset of screen movies that would connect the world with collective trends and messages. Neptune is about ecstasy, either the "high" received through spiritual revelations or the "high" received through drags and alcohol. It is connected with intoxication, art, music, and dancing. Neptune is a lot like Ketu. It rules the illusions of the world, spirituality, and psychic powers.

Rules: Illusions, deception, confusion, denial, drugs, alcohol, fantasies, fog, dreams, romance, glamour, spirituality, higher consciousness, devotion, cults, the ocean, liquids, oil and gas, sensitivity, psychic.

♇ **Pluto:** Pluto was discovered in 1930. At this time the Depression was in full motion. Tyrants of underworld quality controlled the masses. Mafia leaders, gangsters, and dictators like

Hitler and Stalin were rampant. The discovery of atomic energy caused mass destruction and the threat of total human annihilation from the end of World War II. Pluto resembles Rahu.

Rules: Explosiveness, power, control, manipulation, surrender, transformation, underworld, mafia, secrets, obsessions, compulsions, revenge, big money, sex, atomic energy, big government, corruption, birth, death and healing.

With this information many cycles from the past can be studied to understand the future, and therefore make global predictions both political and economic.

Chapter 4
Planetary Cycles

"We are born at a given moment, in a given place, and like vintage years of wine, we have qualities of the year and the season in which we are born."

Carl Jung

As I look into the future planets arrangements for each year, I chart the patterns and then look backwards in time to see what occurred with similar patterns. This will give a good picture of the future trends, and guidance for the economic developments. To determine the global trends the aspect of Jupiter and Saturn to each other and to the outer planets is most important. The faster inner planets determine when the major events, foreseen from the outer planets Jupiter and Saturn, are activated. This indicates the time within the year an event will occur.

Particularly retrogrades of the inner planets (Mercury, Venus, and Mars) flavor the year in terms of the public's focus. Most importantly, the influence that tempers all these cycles are the Lunar Nodes, Rahu and Ketu, which involves the Sun and Moon. They will cause the Solar and Lunar Eclipses within the year, and during the time frames of the eclipses major events occur. The eclipses occur twice a year, six months apart. During the time of an eclipse the Lunar Nodes will seem to station for 2-3 months. During this time crucial events of the year generally occur, such as earth quakes, volcanic eruptions, aggression promoting war and destruction.

The eclipses intensify the planets that are in the same sign with them. This actually means if there is a planet conjunct either Rahu (North Node) or Ketu (South Node) it is basically eclipsed and their power is greatly diminished and will cause problems concerning what this planet rules.

It is cycles with in cycles that determine the emotional climate and economic trends. The cycles of the outer planets, within the cycles of Saturn and Jupiter, and the cycles of the inner faster moving planets within the eclipses reveal our future. The retrograde cycle of planets play into the focus of the masses as well. The signs planets retrograde in become the focus of the public.

To take note of the grand trends of an era look at the major cycles of planets, how often they occur and what they have produced in the past.

Listed below are the conjunctions of these planets in the same sign. The oppositions and squares are important as well. Listed here are the conjunctions and how long till they cycle through the entire zodiac to conjoin again. The sign the conjunction occurs in is significant and will flavor it in a different way. The signs give the planets a certain personality and strength or weakness.

Jupiter and Saturn are conjunct every 20 years. It has been said that when a President of the USA was elected on an even year that they died in office. But of course, President Reagan broke this curse or idea, and President Bush Jr. was elected in 2000 and he did not die in office. Both Presidents did have close calls, President Reagan was shot and almost died and Bush was poisoned in Germany. The point here is that the even numbered years were usually around the time Jupiter and Saturn conjunct.

Jupiter/Saturn 20 years
Jupiter/Uranus 14 years
Jupiter/Neptune 13 years
Jupiter/Pluto 13 years
Saturn/Uranus 45 years
Saturn/Neptune 36 years
Saturn/Pluto 33 years
Uranus/Neptune 171 years
Uranus/Pluto 127 years
Neptune/Pluto 492 years

The amount of time a planet spends in a sign will give an idea how to gauge the speed of a planet in terms of making predictions (this is when a planet is not in a retrograde cycle)

Moon: 2½ days
Sun: 1 month
Mercury: 1 month
Venus: 1 month
Mars: 2 months
Jupiter: 1 year
Saturn: 2½ years
Uranus: 7 years
Neptune: 12 years

Pluto: 12-13 years; currently (Pluto has an elliptical orbit, when furthest from the Sun it can stay in a sign for 30 years).

The year of 2001 was a year of great change and radical shifts. The biggest planetary aspect of that year was Saturn opposed Pluto. Saturn opposes Pluto every 33 years. But the hard aspects between Saturn and Pluto (conjunction, square, opposition) occur 4 times within the 33 year cycle. Saturn will either conjunct, square, or oppose Pluto around 8-9 years. The opposition of Saturn and Pluto means a breakdown of the current old system. The signs that Pluto and Saturn were in are Scorpio (Pluto) and Taurus (Saturn). These signs usually denote money issues, therefore meaning there will be a crises in the economic department globally.

The other important aspect occurring within this time was Jupiter conjunct Rahu which means Jupiter is eclipsed by the Nodes. Jupiter generally refers to the financial climate, Jupiter is money and freedom. Furthermore, Jupiter is in the sign Gemini which is a sign for travel and communications, which did go through a complete overhaul. Boiling it down to the month and day that the event the terrorist attack on America occurred Mars came into an opposition with Jupiter and Rahu. Mars conjoined Ketu, and Ketu rules accidents and Mars rules war, but it was the impending aspect of Saturn opposed Pluto that instigated this event because this is indicates a big shift, and this kind of shift does occur every 8-9 years, when Saturn and Pluto conjunct, square or oppose each other. There is another cycle within this cycle, it was Mars conjunct Ketu and Jupiter conjunct Rahu. Mars/Ketu are opposed Jupiter/Rahu. This means both Jupiter and Mars are eclipsed by the Nodes. The actual trigger for the exact day that it occurred has to do with the Moon. The Moon came into Gemini conjoining Jupiter and Rahu. The Moon is sometimes looked at as the timer of an event of this nature.

<table>
<tr><td>7th h.
♓</td><td>8th h.
♈</td><td>9th h.
♄ 20:52 Roh
♉</td><td>10th h.
☽ 04:12 Mrg
☊ 09:13 Ard
♃ 17:42 Ard
♊</td></tr>
<tr><td>6th h.
♒</td><td colspan="2" rowspan="2">Attack on America
Tue 09-11-2001
08:46:00
New York, NY
USA
Timezone: 5 DST: 1
Latitude: 40N42'51
Longitude: 74W00'23
Ayanamsha : -23:52:34 Lahiri</td><td>11th h.
♀ 24:31 Asl
♋</td></tr>
<tr><td>5th h.
♅ 27:57 Dha
♆ 12:28 Shr
♑</td><td>12th h.
☉ 24:58 PPh
♌</td></tr>
<tr><td>4th h.
☋ 09:13 Mul
♂ 07:34 Mul
♐</td><td>3rd h.
♇ 18:45 Jye
♏</td><td>2nd h.
♎</td><td>1st h.
☿ 20:24 Has
Asc 20:28 Has
♍</td></tr>
</table>

The year of 2008-2009 was a big turning point but 2010 looks even more extreme when figuring out the planetary climate globally.

In 2008 Saturn and Uranus came into an opposition, this opposition occurs 5 times while both planets transit back and forth in their retrograde cycles. In October 2008 Saturn and Uranus came into their 1st opposition and on that time the stock market had a major downturn. This created a major panic. This time was compared to the day the stock market crashed in 1929. Uranus is sudden unexpected change and Saturn is contraction and loss. This was the time of great loss globally for the stock market. In 1929 Saturn was opposed Pluto, and in 2001 many events triggered and began the downfall that finally crashed in 2008. Looking back at the time before when Saturn and Uranus opposed each other was in the late 1960's. The oppositions of Saturn and Uranus occur about every 45 years. The last time this occurred in the late 1960's there was a revolution.

Saturn and Uranus opposed 1967-1969. Saturn was in Pisces and Uranus in Virgo. This time frame will have some similarities to the year of 2008-2010. Looking back at 1967 there was the onset of the hippie era, creativity ran high. This was one the most outstanding years for movie production and music. Progress was made for plans to explore outer space and medical discoveries took a leap. In 1969 the USA put men on the Moon.

There was an explosion of radical visions and eccentric movements much like the radical hippie rebellion. The Internet has united and at the same time isolated people. People from around the world are now in communication with one another,

In the late 1960s events such as Woodstock were seen as an event that united thousands with a message of unity and freedom. It was called the Aquarian Exposition. It was the event that represented freedom and change. The younger generation radically opposed the conservative rigid governmental rule. From the war in Viet Nam, to the racial uprising and sexual liberation, the planets of change transformed our world then and will as well now.

Saturn opposed Uranus activates radical change that opposes the old patterns that no longer work. These are extreme times of change and shifts of energy. The initial opposition was in October 2008 producing a radical shift that set the tone for 2009 and 2010. Uranus in Pisces is concerned with the development of scientific research. Pisces pertains to the final frontiers; information that is out of the box. This will produce an explosion of new discoveries that will ultimately change how we view our universe and medical healing pertaining to energy. Saturn in Virgo indicates medical discoveries and the field of learning and information will explode. Virgo rules the harvest and food. This can mean a breakthrough discovery in agriculture and health. Virgo's rulership of health and healing reflects the massive Health Insurance Plan initiated during this time by President Obama.

Jupiter will conjunct Uranus every 14 years. In 2010 and 2011 Jupiter conjuncts Uranus in Pisces. This will produce excitement and the sudden changes that will be necessary for our growth. This will give us the opportunity to expand our awareness. I have called this the "lottery win aspect." It has the effect of suddenly expanding and changing situations. Watch the sudden spikes in the stock market at these times.

Looking back at the last time Jupiter conjoined Uranus in the sign of Pisces was the year of 1928. To confirm that this is a time of major medical discoveries: Alexander Flemming discovered penicillin in 1928 and changed the world of modem medicine by introducing the age of antibiotics and his discovery of penicillin continues to save millions of lives.

Extreme hurricanes and earthquakes rock the world as this conjunction will produce extreme events. Uranus rules earthquakes and Jupiter's conjunction in a water sign (Pisces) will make events more severe concerning weather and earth changes. There were 2 catastrophic earthquakes with the highest magnitude in 2010 hitting Haiti and Chili.

Another time in history that the planets were in a similar alignment as 2010 was February 1931. There was a grand mutable cross involving the same planets, and Mars was retrograde in Cancer. Saturn was opposed Jupiter and Pluto, squaring Uranus, plus Rahu and Ketu were squaring Saturn and Pluto/Jupiter. This was the time of the great depression and the banks were closing with an insecure financial future. In 2010 Saturn will oppose Uranus/Jupiter, square Pluto, and Rahu and Ketu all in mutable signs. Mars was retrograde in Cancer most of the year the weakest sign (debilitation). Mars in Cancer causes problems for the housing markets. Mars rules Real Estate.

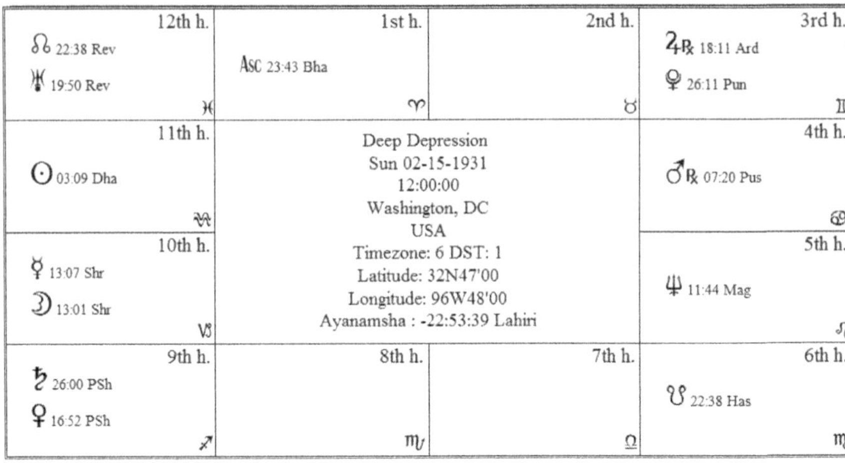
12th h.
☊ 22:38 Rev
♅ 19:50 Rev
♓
1st h.
Asc 23:43 Bha
♈
2nd h.
♉
3rd h.
♃℞ 18:11 Ard
♇ 26:11 Pun
♊
11th h.
☉ 03:09 Dha
♒
Deep Depression
Sun 02-15-1931
12:00:00
Washington, DC
USA
Timezone: 6 DST: 1
Latitude: 32N47'00
Longitude: 96W48'00
Ayanamsha : -22:53:39 Lahiri
4th h.
♂℞ 07:20 Pus
♋
10th h.
☿ 13:07 Shr
☽ 13:01 Shr
♑
5th h.
♆ 11:44 Mag
♌
9th h.
♄ 26:00 PSh
♀ 16:52 PSh
♐
8th h.
♏
7th h.
♎
6th h.
☋ 22:38 Has
♍

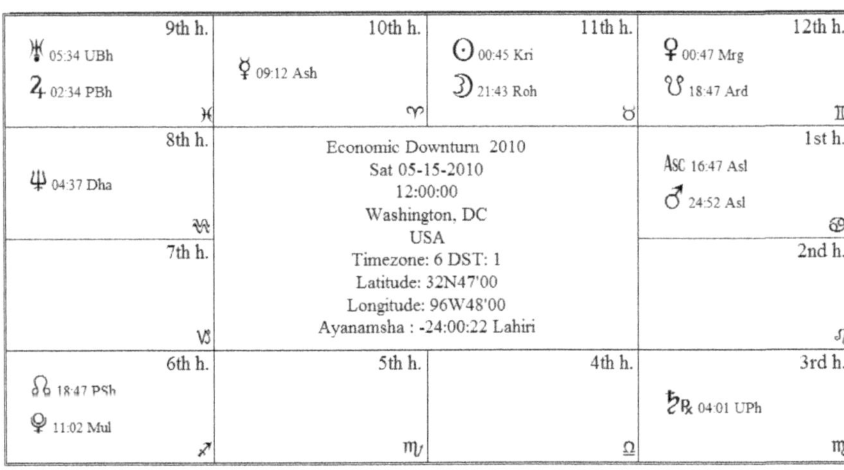
9th h.
♅ 05:34 UBh
♃ 02:34 PBh
♓
10th h.
☿ 09:12 Ash
♈
11th h.
☉ 00:45 Kri
☽ 21:43 Roh
♉
12th h.
♀ 00:47 Mrg
☋ 18:47 Ard
♊
8th h.
♆ 04:37 Dha
♒
Economic Downturn 2010
Sat 05-15-2010
12:00:00
Washington, DC
USA
Timezone: 6 DST: 1
Latitude: 32N47'00
Longitude: 96W48'00
Ayanamsha : -24:00:22 Lahiri
1st h.
Asc 16:47 Asl
♂ 24:52 Asl
♋
7th h.
♑
2nd h.
♌
6th h.
☊ 18:47 PSh
♇ 11:02 Mul
♐
5th h.
♏
4th h.
♎
3rd h.
♄℞ 04:01 UPh
♍

Chapter 5
Past Astrological Timelines Reveal the Future

"A child is born on that day and at that hour when the celestial rays are in mathematical harmony with one's individual karma. The horoscope is a challenging portrait revealing one's unalterable past, and probable future results.

Swami Sri Yukteswar

There are cycles within cycles that determine the trends of each year. The most important cycle that concerns all of life's experiences is the nodal axis of the Moon, called Rahu and Ketu. As mentioned before this is the axis of fate and destiny for Rahu brings us into life and deals with all things in the material world and Ketu pertains to the spiritual world and determines our spiritual development and exit from this world.

Within the nodal axis the other planets that determine the emotional trends globally are the social planets Jupiter and Saturn. These cycles of Rahu/Ketu and Jupiter/Saturn will work together to determine the cyclic patterns of events on planet Earth. Both Rahu and Ketu are diametrically opposite in meanings and results, and Saturn and Jupiter are opposites as well in meaning. Rahu is the material world and Ketu is the spiritual world, and Jupiter is growth and expansion while Saturn is contraction and limitation.

Understanding these simple meanings and understanding those opposite energies create our ups and downs in our world. Looking backwards will give the understanding of these cycles and how they work, so we can apply these results to the future. With this information we can plan for the cyclic trends whether the trends will be up or down. These cycles are the same as the ebb and flow of the tides. There is a time when to move forward and a time to pull back.

With this understanding Rahu is much like Jupiter it expands and increases things and Ketu is like Saturn for it is about withdrawal, loss and contraction. A look at this time line of history in America will reveal this process.

The cycle of Saturn and Jupiter are 20 year cycles. Jupiter and Saturn conjunct each other every 20 years. Jupiter takes 12 years to transit through the entire zodiac of 12 signs, therefore it remains in one sign a year. Saturn takes 30 years to transit through the entire zodiac of 12 signs, but it remains in a sign for 2 *Vi* years. So it takes 20 years for these 2 planets to catch up to each other and form a conjunction. 10 years after the conjunction of Jupiter and Saturn these 2 planets will form an opposition to each other in opposite signs. So we will look at 10 year increments, the conjunction, then the opposition 10 years later, then 10 years later from this last date they return to a conjunction. This 20 year cycle of Jupiter and Saturn is of major importance and is referred to in many cycles of different cultures. The Katoons of Mayan astrology are 20 year increments. And it is speculated that this cycle of 20 years must relate to the Jupiter and Saturn 20 year cycle.

Along with the 20 year cycle of Saturn and Jupiter there is the cycle of Rahu and Ketu which is a revolving axis of 2 points that travel backwards in the zodiac. These 2 points are always exactly opposite. These points travel through the entire zodiac of 12 signs in 18 14 years. So they reach their half way point in about 9 years. They remain in a sign for 1 14 years or 18 months. The half way point of Rahu and Ketu is almost the same as the half cycle of Jupiter and Saturn, when they form an opposition.

The big picture will be revealed with these 20 year and 10 year segments, but to really observe the smaller trends for the stock market involves the break down of these cycles, which are:

9 years is the half cycle of Rahu/Ketu
3-4 years Jupiter will conjoin one of the Nodes (Rahu or Ketu)
6 years Saturn will conjunct one of the nodes (Rahu or Ketu)
At these intersections there will be a rise or fall.

Primarily, Saturn with Rahu gives a rise in the economy and Saturn with Ketu will cause a decline. Jupiter with Rahu can go either way, and Jupiter with Ketu can go either way as well. What really determines the true rise will be the signs that Saturn and Jupiter are in. When Jupiter is in its sign of exaltation (Cancer) it will give a quick strong rise especially with the nodes, and Saturn in it's sign of rulership or exaltation (Capricorn, Aquarius, and Libra) there will be building and productivity. Mark the times when Jupiter is in Cancer and Saturn is in Capricorn there was always a rise in the economy. Generally, with a rise there is usually an over extension and things become imbalanced, and the economy has to retreat after these high times.

These points are to be tracked in the economic cycles globally, the 20 year cycle of Jupiter's and Saturn's conjunction, and the half way point between this 20 years where they oppose each 10 years after the conjunction. Then about a year and a half following the conjunction or opposition of Jupiter and Saturn, both Jupiter and Saturn will cross over the nodal axis.

1) Jupiter conjunct Saturn 20 years
2) Jupiter opposed Saturn 10 years after the conjunction
3) Within the conjunction and opposition of Jupiter and Saturn their crossing over the nodes of the Moon (Rahu and Ketu) create the shifts.

This demonstration is how these cycles relate to the highs and lows in the economy.

1920-1929 The roaring twenties were in full gear in the early 1920's. Usually, there is a time of great expansion right before there is a time of sudden collapse due to the extreme rapid growth from overextension. In the early 1920's there was very rapid growth, the auto industry stimulated rapid growth in many areas such as oil, glass, and road building, tourism, a boom in construction, offices, factories, and homes.

1920-1922 Jupiter and Saturn conjoined in Leo and Virgo. In 1922 both Jupiter and Saturn conjoined Rahu in Virgo. During this time the economy was on a roll expanding beyond its means.

1929-1931, ten years later when Jupiter and Saturn opposed each other there was the biggest crash of the stock market in the 20th century, October 1929, this caused the Great Depression. The Federal Reserve made no effort to intervene and it was impossible to get a loan. President Hoover passed a massive tax increase which made things worse, and by 1932 the unemployment rate was 23.6%. The lowest point of this depression was the winter of 1932. But from this low point the economy began to make a comeback and grew (58%) to 1937. During the opposition of Jupiter and Saturn in 1930, Jupiter was in Gemini and Saturn was in Sagittarius. There were no conjunctions of the nodes (Rahu/Ketu) during this time. It wasn't until Jupiter conjoined Ketu in 1933 that the downward spiral began to reverse during these depressing times. Then Saturn conjoined Rahu in 1934, resulting in an increase in the economy.

1940-1949 Saturn and Jupiter made their 20 year cycle to form a conjunction in Aries and in 1941 they both conjunct Ketu. Here they are making a conjunction and both cross over Ketu this time instead of Rahu which was the place they crossed 20 years ago. In this case Saturn does not fare well with Ketu especially in its sign of debilitation. The next 10 years was one of the most destructive times on our planet, World War II. Actually, the war made the economy better, for they needed to build products for the war.

1950-1951 Ten years later in 1950 Jupiter and Saturn moved into their opposition where Saturn crossed over Ketu and Jupiter crossed over Rahu by 1951. Jupiter was in Aquarius and Saturn was in Leo. The 1950's had economic growth. This was a readjustment period for the war had ended and this was a time of building a new life. Jupiter crossing over Rahu can sometimes cause expansion but Saturn crossing of Ketu is not good for expansion. The signs for Jupiter and Saturn were not conducive to rapid growth.

1960-1961 Jupiter conjuncts Saturn in Sagittarius and then Capricorn where they both cross over Ketu. During this time President John F. Kennedy passed the largest tax cut in history and during 1963-1969 there was great growth but things started slowing down in the late 1960's. Jupiter and Saturn both cross over Ketu in 1962 which is not a great time but the fact that Saturn was in Capricorn gave it great strength to build things, in which there was economic growth. There was great strife during this time, President Kennedy was assassinated in 1963 and the racial strife and tension in the world was very destructive from 1964-69.

1969-1971 Jupiter opposed Saturn and Jupiter conjoined Ketu and Saturn conjoined Rahu. Jupiter opposed Saturn in 1970, Saturn was in Aries and Jupiter in Libra. Saturn was in its debilitation sign which causes a depletion of its ability to build up the economy. From the 1970s' inflation and unemployment rose sharply. The United States grew increasingly dependent on oil importation, resulting in oil supply shocks in 1973 and 1979. Both of those years Jupiter conjoined Rahu, Jupiter conjoined Rahu in 1973 in Sagittarius and in 1979 Jupiter conjoined Rahu in Leo. Jupiter does not do well with Rahu. This means Jupiter is eclipsed by Rahu. President Nixon closed the gold window at the Federal Reserve, taking the United States entirely off the gold standard. In 1974, productivity shrunk by 1.5%, though this soon recovered.

1979-1980 Jupiter and Saturn conjoined in Leo with Rahu, and during the next 10 years there were many changes that increased debts but expanded the economy. In 1981, Ronald Reagan introduced Reaganomics, expansive economic policies, cutting marginal federal income tax rates by 25%. Inflation dropped dramatically. During the Reagan Administration the gap between those in the upper socioeconomic levels and those in the lower socioeconomic levels increased and the national debt tripled reaching record levels. It is safe to say this was a time of expansion. Jupiter and Saturn together with Rahu in Leo indicate an increase.

1989-1990 Saturn and Jupiter opposed each other, Jupiter in Cancer conjoined Ketu, and Saturn conjoined Rahu in Capricorn. During the next 10 years there was a boom in the stock market. From 1994 to 2000 real output increased, inflation was manageable and unemployment dropped to below 5%, resulting in a soaring stock market known as the Dot-com boom. By 2000, however, it was evident a bubble in stock valuations *had* occurred, such that beginning in March 2000. Jupiter in the sign of Cancer is all about prosperity and expansion. Saturn moves into Capricorn which is Saturn's sign of rulership increasing Saturn's ability to build the economy. This was a time of major expansion for these 10 years. But too much expansion creates a need to pull back later.

2000-2002 Jupiter conjoined Saturn, and Rahu in Gemini was around the time of the terrorist attack on America. Although the economic drop during the next 10 years was blamed on this event there were many other blooming effects that originated in the late 1990s, the housing markets lent money to many who could not afford these loans later, these effects came down around 2007-2008. Here we have another depression that occurred due to over expansion that occurred earlier. But this time the government *did* intervene, if they didn't it would have been just like the Great Depression.

2010-2012 Jupiter and Saturn oppose, and Jupiter conjoins Ketu and Saturn crosses Rahu. This astrological pattern is very much like the pattern that occurred in 1931 during the rock bottom level of the Great Depression. There is a grand mutable cross in both these charts involving the same patterns. The planets involved in the Grand Cross in mutable signs are the same but in different signs. This time frame 2010-2012 will go down in history as the most destructive and volatile.

Charts on p.33, 1931 Deep Depression and 2010 Economic Downturn

In the chart of 1931 the same planets that form a grand cross are in the mutable signs all aspecting each other forming a grand square or cross. A Grand square or a grand cross means there are 4 planets that square each other in angles from one another. These planets will form 2 oppositions with these same planets and form a cross. The Moon's nodes (Rahu and Ketu) are in the mutable signs, Rahu in Pisces and Ketu in Virgo. Rahu is conjunct Uranus in Pisces in the 2010 chart. In 1931 Uranus was in Pisces just as it is in the 2010 chart. Uranus takes about 84 years to make a complete revolution through the entire zodiac.

Jupiter and Saturn are in opposition in 1931 in the mutable signs Gemini and Sagittarius. In 2010 they are opposed in mutable signs Pisces and Virgo.

Saturn is opposed Pluto in 1931 and Saturn is square Pluto in 2010. So the comparison of these 2 charts emulate the similar planetary relationships and the results are similar and for both these time periods had massive losses in housing, jobs, banks and the same overall disposition of the economy. Mars was even retrograde in Cancer in 1931 where it was retrograde for most of the year in Cancer in 2010. Mars was retrograde but remained in Cancer from October 2009 till May 2010. Again, Mars rules real estate and when a planet is retrograde and in a sign of debilitation it will cause trouble in the areas the planet rules.

The next 10 years will be a slow recovery as it was from 1931-1940. There are many shifts and changes that have to be implemented to create growth in a bottomed out economy. Just as President Hoover passed a massive tax increase during this time, so has President Obama passed a tax reform that will increase taxes.

2010 -2012 The polarity of the political and religious issues during this time prevents growth on many levels. Many events that will change the awareness on a huge scale will take place after 2012 leading to a new world. The following years will lead to expansion and discoveries that give a new perspective and progressive growth within the economy. The prospect of war is always on the edge and can manifest all the more within these next 10 years as it did between the years leading into the 1940's.

2020-2021 Jupiter is conjunct Saturn in Sagittarius and then in Capricorn with Ketu. In 1960- 1961 Jupiter and Saturn were conjunct in Sagittarius and both crossed over Ketu. This should produce a similar effect as it did during these years. In which there was steady growth and expansion during that time. There will be expansion but the growth will depend on over expansion in ways that will cause problems later. The imbalance will be felt by the next opposition in 2030. Saturn in Capricorn will create a stability based on false images. Saturn is strong in Capricorn especially for leadership and government, but Ketu with Saturn causes Saturn to falter for it is not based on a steady foundation.

2030-2031 Saturn and Jupiter will oppose in the signs Taurus and Scorpio. Saturn is in Taurus conjunct Ketu and Jupiter is in Scorpio with Rahu. This is will produce a very mixed result since Jupiter is eclipsed by Rahu and Saturn does not fare well with Ketu. The signs Scorpio and Taurus relate to money issues. When both Jupiter and Saturn conjoined in Taurus in 2000 the financial market began a steady downward trend. But Jupiter in Scorpio is positive and Saturn fares well in Taurus. The signs are good for the planets but the combination with Rahu and Ketu cause problems. Certain business will prosper while others falter. The economy is making a major shift from the traditional banks to something that has not yet been created.

2040-2041 Jupiter and Saturn conjunct in Libra with Ketu, Jupiter does not prosper in Libra but Saturn is all powerful in the sign of exaltation Libra, so it will benefit the economy. The growth will be slow and steady since both planets are conjunct Ketu. Libra is the sign of balance creating a consciousness of unity that unites the political parties. This positive development will enable growth that will continue and develop the Golden years ahead.

2050-2051 Jupiter and Saturn will oppose each other, Jupiter will be in Cancer and Saturn will be in Capricorn. This is the best possible placement for these 2 planets in opposition because Saturn is its sign of rulership and Jupiter is exalted in Cancer, additionally Rahu and Ketu are not in conjunction with these placements which gives both Jupiter and Saturn the opportunity to perform to their highest capacity. This will be a very fruitful and prosperous era. After many years of ups and downs this will be a very happy, peaceful time globally. There is a sense of unity and togetherness. The world has progressed and grown to a higher consciousness.

It is cycles within cycles Rahu/Ketu and Jupiter/Saturn that produce the many changing tides within the framework of our society and lives. It is not only just the patterns and cycles these planets form but it is also important to understand what signs these planets occupy, for the signs can make the energy better or worse. This is another layer to this complex web of life. But there is a synergy and pattern that can be recognized and used for the understanding and betterment of our lives.

Chapter 6

Is there Money in my Chart?

"Billionaire's Charts"
"Anyone can be a millionaire, but to become a billionaire, you need an astrologer. "

J.P. Morgan, founder of Morgan Bank

Let's face it, the question that is presented the very most to an astrologer is about FINANCES. Actually to find money in a chart is very simple. There are some very specific rules that will predict if one will have a wealthy life, full of riches. These rules will apply to those whom the money comes naturally. To understand what it is in a chart that creates massive wealth will give clues to the money combinations which can be later activated through the transits in our own charts. Let us prove these points through the mega wealthy. What makes a billionaire's chart? The charts will tell us how!

Planets

There are certain planets that rule wealth and money. They are specifically Jupiter and Venus. These two planets are the great natural benefics, meaning they are the two most positive planets that produce luck, wealth, luxury and comforts. These are actually called the karakas (indicators) for wealth and prosperity.

Planets for Prosperity and Money:

Sun: CEOs, Presidents, Bosses, Power Father, Gold

Moon: Public, Fame, Mother, Silver, Water

Mercury: Communications, Media, Advertising, Trade, Sales, Travel

Venus: Luxuries such as Cars, Boats, Airplanes, Opulent Wealth

Mars: Real Estate, Engineers, Intelligence, Siblings

Jupiter: Luck, Fortune, Freedom, Money, Teaching, Philanthropy, Travel

Saturn, Land, Cattle, Trusts, Government

Uranus: Change, Electricity, Airplanes, Computers

Neptune; Oil, Water, Oceans, Prescription and Illegal Drugs, Alcohol, Films, Movies, and Photography

Pluto: Big Business, Monopolies, Mafia, Control and Power Rahu: Magnifies the planets that it aspects, especially a conjunction.

Ketu: Depletes the planets that it aspects, especially the conjunction. Can give psychic intuitive powers (used in business).

- Rahu and Ketu can sometimes give great wealth when with a planet that is powerful by sign. For example: Ketu with Venus, and Venus is in its sign of rulership or exalted will produce big wealth.

Houses

There are 12 houses and each represent an area of your life. The next specific thing to look for is what houses in your natal chart are going to produce money.

The houses for money are 2,11, 9, 5 and 8.

The 2nd house rules your income and financial matters in your life. How you earn your money.

The 11th house is the house of great gains, and pertains to large sums of money that come in all at once.

The 9th house is the house of luck and fortune.

The 5th house is the house of speculation and intelligence. It pertains to how one gains from stocks, trading, and creative pursuits and talent.

The 8th house is the house of inheritance, meaning money that comes through others, not your own earnings.

The 1st house represents YOU, so when you have connections with any of these other wealth producing houses with the 1st house this means the money is brought specifically to you.

Rulership

Planets take rulership over a sign. There are 5 planets that rule 2 signs and the Sun and Moon rule 1 sign each. The outer planets Uranus, Neptune and Pluto do not rule signs.

Sun rules Leo

Moon rules Cancer

Mercury rules Gemini and Virgo

Venus rules Taurus and Libra

Mars rules Aries and Scorpio

Jupiter rules Sagittarius and Pisces

Saturn rules Capricorn and Aquarius

To see wealth in a chart you must find the signs on these money houses. **The planets that rule houses 2, 11, 5 and 9 are your money planets.** The ruler of the 8th house will not bring you money, but planets placed in that house can indicate money through inheritance or marriage. Planets in houses 2, 11, 5 and 9 will produce money, but if you do not have planets in these houses the planetary rulers of these houses will indicate the capability to achieve money, and from what source.

*The most powerful combination for money is when the 2nd house is connected to the 11th house. It means money will come in large sums. This means the planetary ruler of the 2nd house is in the 11th house, or the 11th house ruling planet is in the 2nd house. Any connection of the 2nd house with the 11th house will create money.

*The next powerful combination is when the 1st house is connected to the 2nd house. This means the planetary ruler of the 1st house is in the 2nd house, or the 2nd house ruler is in the 1st house. Any connection of the 1st house to the 2nd house will create money.

Combinations of the wealth producing houses will bring money, and this means any connection between the 2, 5, 9, and the 11 houses produce money. When they are connected to the 1st house, the money is brought to YOU. In Vedic astrology this combination or connection of these houses are called Dhana Yogas. But let's just keep it simple and relate to them as combining the money houses for they do create money in a chart and a person's life.

Houses: How you Make Money

1st House: You
2nd House: Money you earn, salary, income
3rd House: Travel, communications, teaching and writing, siblings
4th House: Real estate, property, land, cars, luxury items such as boats and airplanes, mother
5th House: Speculation, stock market, sports, entertainment, intelligence, children, grandfather
6th House: Medical career, healing, restaurants, food, service, employees, aunts/uncles
7th House: Marriage, business partners, grandmother
8th House: Inheritance, partner's wealth, insurance, taxes
9th House: Travel, teaching, luck, fortune, publishing, law, lawyers, father
10th House: Career, social standing, reputation, government
11th House: Great gains, money produced from career, fulfillment of desires, friends
12th House: Charity, non-profit organizations, places of retirement, film, losses

Earth Signs and Houses

The natural Earth houses 2, 6, and 10 will be active as well for financial gains. In the natural zodiac the earth signs are Taurus, Virgo and Capricorn. In the natural zodiac Taurus is the 2nd sign, Virgo the 6th sign and Capricorn the 10th sign. These houses are specifically about earthly matters, which pertain to money. The 2nd house is the money you earn, the 6th house is your work on a daily bases, and the 10th house is your career. In Vedic astrology these houses are called the Artha houses and pertain to your materialistic well being on this planet. So the Earth signs and the earth houses (2, 6 and 10) are indicators for money and wealth in a chart.

The planet that rules the 2nd house of money will indicate the area you will be most successful in making money. The house this planet resides in gives clues to financial success. For example; if you have the ruler of the 2nd house in the 3rd house you could make your money through travel, teaching or writing.

The planet that rules the 11th house will indicate where our fortunes can come.

Next step is to look at the aspects and combinations of planets in the chart. The aspects are the degree orbs between 2 planets. Certain degree orbs are more fortunate than others, some create ease and luck while others create tension and obstacles for the planets involved. The aspect that gives wealth and ease is the trine, 120 degree between planets, conjunctions and oppositions are important too.

Combinations of the planets that rule the money houses will produce money. This means that if the rulers of these money houses are combined in any way they will produce money. The way the money is achieved is through the house these planets occupy, meaning if they occupy the 5th house money can come through speculation, sports, or entertainment. If a combination is in the 8th house the money may come from and inheritance.

Combinations of planets that rule 2nd, 11th, 5th and 9th houses will produce great wealth, and if Jupiter aspects these planets it will magnify the results of wealth and money even more. Jupiter expands what it aspects. Jupiter's aspects are the conjunction, opposition and the trine aspect (120 degrees).

To predict *when* these planets will produce their results, the transits of the planets in the heavens as they aspect the natal combinations produce their results.

Venus is the planet that produces great wealth. Venus rules luxuries in life. To have a life of lavish wealth you must have a good Venus in your chart. In Vedic astrology there is a yoga in a chart that depicts great wealth. If someone has this combination they do have great money and wealth. Bill Gates has a perfect Lakshmi yoga. With Lakshmi yoga the first and foremost thing required is Venus must be in one of these three signs in the chart: which is Taurus, Libra or Pisces. These signs are the strongest signs for Venus to be in, for Venus rules both Taurus and Libra and it is exalted (strongest) in Pisces. The other parameters are that the ruling planet (planet that rules the 1st house/Ascendant) must be strong (by sign and house it is in) and this planet must be aspected by the planet that rules the 9th house or connected to the 9th house. Some say, that the Ascendant ruler must be strong, and the 9th house planet must be strong and Venus is in Taurus, Libra or Pisces. The difference is that the 1st house ruler doesn't have to connect to the 9th house ruler.

To be a strong planet it must be in a strong sign, in a good house and not aspected by more than one malefic planet.

Good houses: the best are 1, 5, 9 and the angular houses 1, 4, 7, and 10 are powerful and will promote a person to power and success. The signs a planet are strong in are, their exaltation sign and the sign they rule. The weakest sign a planet can be in is the debilitation sign.

The natural malefic planets are: Sun, Mars, Saturn, and Rahu, and Ketu.
Natural benefics are: Venus, Jupiter, Mercury and Moon

- A rule to remember, Venus is the only planet that prospers well in the 12th house: and Venus in the 12th will bring wealth and money. The stronger by sign the better the wealth. Venus is strongest in Pisces then Libra and Taurus

Exaltation is the strongest sign and Debilitation is the weakest sign for these Planets

Exaltation /Debilitation
Sun - Aries/Libra 10 degrees
Moon - Taurus/Scorpio 3 degrees
Mercury - Virgo/Pisces 15 degrees
Venus - Pisces/Virgo 27 degrees
Mars - Capricorn/Cancer 28 degrees
Jupiter - Cancer/Capricorn 5 degrees
Saturn - Libra/Aries 20 degrees

Aspects

There are certain aspects in Vedic astrology that are considered full aspects meaning they give 100 percent power so they are the ones to denote. An aspect is considered as it aspects the entire sign, not just a degree orb.

Planets full aspect:

Sun, Moon, Mercury, Venus:

0 degrees Conjunction (1/1) in the same sign.

180 degrees, Opposition (7/7) seven signs from each other.

*These full aspects are counted forward only in the chart.
*The forward motion in the Vedic chart is clockwise.
*All planets aspect in conjunction and opposition only the planets below also have their own special full aspect.

Mars: (4/8) 4 signs and 8 signs forward
Saturn: (3/10) 3 signs and 10 signs forward
Jupiter: (5/9) 5 signs and 9 signs forward
Rau/Ketu: (5/9) 5 signs and 9 signs forward

- Rahu and Ketu as they aspect another planet can have the effect of Jupiter aspecting a planet for they will expand and inflate things. Particularly, if Rahu is in the main houses of money (2, 5, 9, and 11) Rahu in the 2nd and the 11th is especially powerful for wealth.
- When Rahu or Ketu aspect Jupiter with a trine then Jupiter mutually aspects them with a trine. This in another powerful indication of extremes and multiplies a person's wealth!

These aspects are connectors of the planets.

* Another rule is that in Vedic astrology the planets will aspect the houses even though there may not be a planet there. When a planet aspects a house that it rules, it will empower the house for what that house is good for.

For example; If Mars is in Libra in the 8th house then Mars aspects the 2nd house by opposition (7/7) and the 2nd house has Aries as the sign on the 2nd house, then Mars is aspecting a house that it rules meaning it will empower that house and produce what the 2nd house rules which is money for the person.

Nakshatras

In the system of Vedic astrology there are 27 nakshatras. They are used like the signs. They have specific portions of the zodiac which are 13 degrees and 20 minutes. The signs are 30 degree portions. The nakshatras that pertain to money in a chart are listed here.

The main Nakshatras referenced in text books for wealth and money are:

Purva Phalguni: 13 degrees 20 minutes Leo- 26 degrees 40 minutes Leo
Dhanishta: 23 degrees 20 minutes Capricorn- 6 degrees 40 minutes Aquarius
Uttara Bhadrapada: 3 degrees 20 minutes- 16 degrees 40 minutes Pisces
Revati: 16 degrees 20 minutes- 30 degrees Pisces

* Both Purva Phalguni and Uttara Bhadrapada indicate inheritance.

- I found certain nakshatras to be more prevalent in the charts of the ultra rich, **billionaire's** charts. They are in the **signs of Libra and Scorpio.**

  Jyeshta: 16 degrees 40 minutes-30 Degrees Scorpio
  Vishaka: 20 degrees Libra-3 degrees 20 minutes Scorpio
  Swati: 6 degrees 40 minutes- 20 degrees Libra

Charts of the mega rich will demonstrate all these simple rules presented here: The houses 2, 5, 9, 11 and the 8th house (for money through others).

The connection of the 1st house brings the wealth to the person. The aspects and planets connect and empower these houses of money and wealth.

1st h.	2nd h.	3rd h.	4th h.
☊ 18:56 Rev ASC 08:41 UBh ♓	♈	♄℞ 08:39 Kri ♉	♇ 07:04 Ard ♊
12th h. ♒	Barbara Hutton Thu 11-14-1912 14:25:00 New York, NY New York USA Timezone: 5 DST: 0 Latitude: 40N42'51 Longitude: 74W00'23 Ayanamsha : -22:38:21 Lahiri		5th h. ♆ 03:18 Pun ♋
11th h. ♅ 07:25 USh ☽ 06:11 USh ♑			6th h. ♌
10th h. ♀ 03:12 Mul ♐	9th h. ☿ 20:58 Jye ♃ 26:19 Jye ♏	8th h. ♂ 26:25 Vis ☉ 29:26 Vis ♎	7th h. ☋ 18:56 Has ♍

Barbra Hutton inherited over 100 million from her family, her grandfather made his fortune from the dime store chain Woolworths. She was extravagant with her spending especially concerning love. She was known to flaunt her wealth and buy her way into and out of relationships. She married seven times to the likes of European royalty and Hollywood movie stars, the most noted was Cary Grant. She was very conscientious about her beauty and struggled her entire life to be very thin through surgery and starvation. Her only son Lance died in a plane crash at age 36. She had all that money could buy but happiness seemed to be a fleeting thing she tried desperately to capture.

Planet Jupiter is in her 9th house, the house of fortune, luck and her father. It also aspects Saturn by opposition, and Saturn rules the 11th house of great gains. The Moon ruler of the 5th house of speculation and intelligence is in the 11th house of gains. The Moon aspects the 5th house and rules the 5th house empowering this great money house. And it is also the house of the grandfather (9th house from the 9th house, the father's father). Mars rules her 2nd house of money and the 9th house of luck and fortune and is in the 8th house of inheritances. It is close to the Sun which is the indicator of the father. Mars in the 8th house rules the 2nd house and aspects the 2nd house in opposition (7/7). Jupiter the planet of wealth and luck aspects the 1st house, this brings the luck and wealth to her. Jupiter and Rahu aspect each other and both are indicators of expansion.

Her ascendant degree is in the nakshatra Uttara Bhadrapada the nakshatra of wealth from inheritance, and Rahu is in Revati.

Barbara Hutton has 4 planets in the nakshatras of the mega rich: Mars and the Sun are in Libra, in the nakshatra Vishakha and her Jupiter and Mercury are in Scorpio in the nakshatra Jyeshta.

<table>
<tr><td>5th h.
☊ 18:53 Rev
♓</td><td>6th h.
☽ 10:14 Ash
♈</td><td>7th h.
♄℞ 08:01 Kri
♉</td><td>8th h.
♇ 06:56 Ard
♊</td></tr>
<tr><td>4th h.
♒</td><td colspan="2" rowspan="2">Doris Duke
Fri 11-22-1912
07:30:00
New York, NY
USA
Timezone: 5 DST: 0
Latitude: 40N42'51
Longitude: 74W00'23
Ayanamsha : -22:38:21 Lahiri</td><td>9th h.
♆ 03:13 Pun
♋</td></tr>
<tr><td>3rd h.
♅ 07:41 USh
♑</td><td>10th h.
♌</td></tr>
<tr><td>2nd h.
♀ 12:37 Mul
♐</td><td>1st h.
♂ 01:50 Vis
☉ 07:13 Anu
♅ 14:04 Anu
♃ 28:00 Jye
☿ 29:03 Jye
♏</td><td>12th h.
♎</td><td>11th h.
☋ 18:53 Has
♍</td></tr>
</table>

Doris Duke acquired a fortune of 1.2 Billion at age 25 from her father who founded the American Tobacco Company and Duke Power Company. Her father endowed a small college with millions just to have it named after him, Duke University. Doris was an only child of her father and was highly protected. She was awkwardly tall and extremely beautiful. It was ingrained in her that no one would marry her for anything but her money.

She was married three times and had a premature child who died soon after birth. But her worse controversy appeared over her search for the fountain of youth and spirituality. She adopted a 31 year old Hare Krishna devotee, Chandi. She believed she was in reincarnation of her premature daughter. Chandi took control of her money and her life, and in the end Doris died fearful of all her employees particularly the Butler who Chandi brought in.

Jupiter is in the 1st house and rules the 2nd house of money (Sagittarius), which brings the money to her. Venus the planet of luxuries is in the 2nd house. Jupiter aspects the 5th house and Rahu, and rules the 5th house (Pisces). Jupiter and Rahu are both about expansion and extremes and frequently aspect each other when one is extremely rich. Jupiter also aspects the 9th house of luck, fortune and her father.

Jupiter is conjunct Mercury in the 1st house, and Mercury rules the 8th house of inheritance and the 11 house of gains. Mars is ruler of the 1st house and it is in the 1st house, this empowers her.

Jupiter as ruler of the 2nd house is in the 1st house and is conjunct Mercury the ruler of the 11th house (Virgo). She has all together the connection of the 2nd house and the 11th house in the 1st house. This is the most powerful combination of money ruler of the 1st with the 2nd, and ruler of the 2nd house with the ruler of the 11th house. The fact that these combinations are in the 1st house brings the money to her!

She has her Rahu in the nakshatra Revati for wealth.

The most powerful nakshatras for money are here, Doris Duke has Mars in Vishakha and Jupiter and Mercury in Jyeshta.

Notice the similarities between Doris Dukes' and Barbara Hutton's chart. They were born eight days apart and had similar lives.

12th h.	1st h.	2nd h.	3rd h.
♀ 16:08 UBh ♓	Asc 23:44 Bha ♈	♉	♇ 17:39 Ard ♊
11th h. ♅ 23:45 PBh ☋ 09:22 Sat ☉ 07:55 Sat ♒	Gloria Vanderbilt Wed 02-20-1924 09:55:00 New York, Ny USA Timezone: 5 DST: 0 Latitude: 40N42'51 Longitude: 74W00'23 Ayanamsha : -22:47:44 Lahiri		4th h. ♆ 25:53 Asl ♋
10th h. ☿ 16:03 Shr ♑			5th h. ☽ 07:17 Mag ☊ 09:22 Mag ♌
9th h. ♐	8th h. ♃ 24:03 Jye ♂ 27:34 Jye ♏	7th h. ♄℞ 09:27 Swa ♎	6th h. ♍

Gloria Vanderbilt is an American entrepreneur and heiress She was the heiress of the Vanderbilt fortune. Her father Reginald Vanderbilt died from alcoholism when she was an infant. Gloria was called "poor little rich girl" during the 1930s.due to a custody battle between her mother Gloria Morgan and her aunt Gertrude Vanderbilt Whitney.

After her father's death, her mother was never there to care for her so she attached herself to the hired nanny. When her mother heard her call the nanny "Mother", she was immediately fired. Gloria resented her mother. For her nanny was the only one she knew and loved as a child. In adult life Gloria had four marriages and four children. In the first marriage she was too young, and in the second marriage her husband was 40 years older. Her last marriage was the happiest to writer Wyatt Copper, but she was widowed in 1978. She was very artistic and established herself as a one of America's top fashion designers.

Jupiter ruler of the 9th house (luck fortune and father) is in the 8th house of inheritance, with Mars ruler of the 8th house of inheritance. This simply means she received a powerful inheritance from her father. Mars rules the 1st house (her) therefore, is the ruler of her chart and it is conjunct money producing Jupiter. Jupiter in the 8th house aspects her 2nd house of money. Jupiter aspects Venus in the 12th house, these are the 2 planets that represent wealth. Plus, Venus is in Pisces in the 12th house. Venus is the only planet that denotes wealth in the 12th house plus it is in its most powerful sign Pisces. Venus rules the 2nd house and the fact that it is exalted brings powerful wealth. Venus is in the nakshatra of Uttara Bhadrapada the nakshatra of wealth through inheritance.

Saturn rules the 11th house of great gains and is exalted. Meaning the potential for great gains is high. Ketu in the 11th house in Aquarius aspects Saturn in the 7th house, this connects the 11th house to exalted Saturn ruler of the 11th house.

The Sun in the 11th house aspects the 5th house connecting the 11th house (gains) to the 5th house (speculation). Since the Sun rules the 5th house (Leo) it empowers this house to produce good results.

Her Venus is in the nakshatra Uttara Bhadrapada, indicating money from inheritance.

Gloria Vanderbilt has Mars and Jupiter in the money producing nakshatra Jyestha and Saturn in Swati.

10th h. ☽ 14:33 UBh ♓	11th h. ♈	12th h. ☋ 24:53 Mrg ♉	1st h. ASC 24:58 Pun ♊
9th h. ♒	Bill Gates Fri 10-28-1955 21:15:00 Seattle, WA USA Timezone: 8 DST: 0 Latitude: 47N36'23 Longitude: 122W19'51 Ayanamsha : -23:14:40 Lahiri		2nd h. ♅ 09:02 Pus ♋
8th h. ♑			3rd h. ♃ 04:32 Mag ♇ 05:06 Mag ♌
7th h. ♐	6th h. ☊ 24:53 Jye ♏	5th h. ♆ 04:59 Cht ☉ 11:15 Swa ♀ 26:56 Vis ♄ 28:20 Vis ♎	4th h. ♂ 16:51 Has ☿ 23:19 Has ♍

Bill Gates has achieved his own wealth through his skills as a pioneer in the development of computers. His company Microsoft went public in 1986 and by 1991 he was one of the richest men in the world amassing 4.4 billion dollars. His dad was a lawyer and his mom a teacher. He went to Harvard to become a lawyer but after reading about the first microcomputer the Altair 8800 he and a friend built their first computer in 1975 in their Harvard dorm. He dropped out of school to form his company Microsoft.

He married a business executive, Melinda French. They have three children. Bill and Melinda have donated 22 Billion to the "Bill and Melinda Gates Foundation" that provides international vaccinations and children's health programs, the largest philanthropic contribution to this day. He has been topping the charts as the richest man in the world currently.

The ruler of the chart Mercury (rules the 1st house) is exalted giving him power. It is with the ruler of the 11th (Mars) which brings great gains to him. The Moon ruler of the 2nd house is aspected by opposition to both Mercury and Mars, Mars rules the 11th house of great gains, and Mercury ruler of the 1st house (him). Mars aspects the 11th house by its 8th aspect and it rules the 11th house of Aries, empowering him even more for gains.

Jupiter aspects both the 7th house (great business partners), and 11th house (gains).

Venus is the trump card, for it forms a perfect Lakshmi yoga. Venus is in its own sign of rulership (Libra) and the 1st house ruler Mercury is strong because it is in an angular house (4th house) and it is exalted. The last requirement for Lakshmi Yoga is that the 9th house ruler (Saturn) be in a strong house and it must be in a strong sign. Saturn is exalted (Libra) in the 5th house. Venus ruler of the 5th house is in its own sign (Libra) and Saturn ruler of the 9th house of luck and fortune is exalted in the 5th house of speculation. These 2 powerful planets connect the lucky 9th with the fortunate 5th houses with their conjunction in the 5th house. Additionally, all the planets in the 5th house: Sun, Venus and Saturn aspect the 11th house of gains by opposition. The 5th house is the house of intelligence and he made his fortune from his brilliant mind.

He has his Moon in the nakshatra Uttara Bhadrapada one of the nakshatras for great wealth.

Bill Gates has 4 planets in the money producing nakshatras of the mega rich, Sun in Swati, Venus and Saturn in Vishakha, and Rahu in Jyeshta.

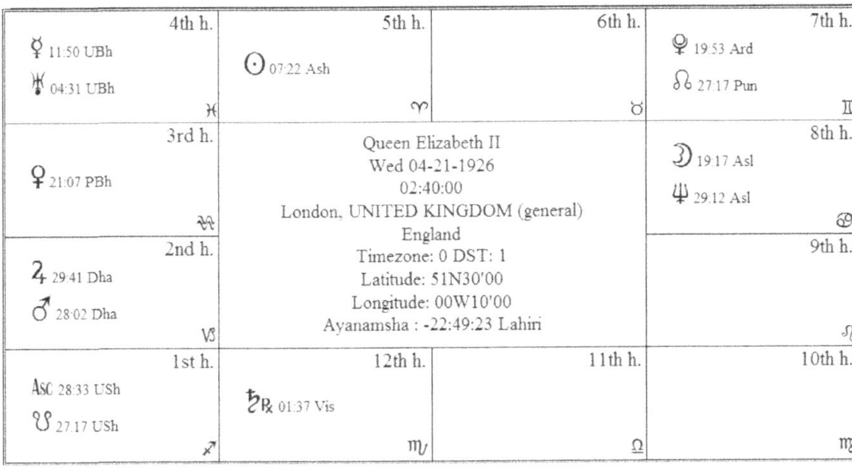

Queen Elizabeth was born into the monarchy where opulent wealth is a way of life. She became the Queen at age 25 upon the death of her father king George IV. At age 11, the eldest daughter to George IV, Elizabeth became heir to the British throne. She was the richest woman in the world during her rein.

She married Prince Phillip of Greece in 1947 and celebrated their 50th wedding anniversary in 1997. They have four Royal offspring. Her role is to symbolize the unity of the Commonwealth of Nations.

Her second house of money has the great benefic Jupiter ruler of the 1st house, but it is weaker due to its debilitation sign, but because it is with Mar in its exaltation, and the exact degree of exaltation the debilitated Jupiter becomes empowered. Jupiter rules the 1st house and Mars rules the 5th house of speculation and the mind. Whenever Mars is associated with the 5th house of the mind Mars denotes a high degree of intelligence. The Sun is also exalted in the 5th house and it rules the 9th house of luck and fortune. The 2nd house has Mars the ruler of the 5th house and the Sun in the 5th house rules the 9th house. This is a remarkable connection of the 2nd, 5th and 9th houses. Also, Mars aspects the 5th house and it rules the 5th house (Aries), empowering the 5th house of intelligence. Both Mars and Jupiter aspect the 8th house and the Moon which is in the 8th house which to also rules the 8th house (Cancer). Her 8th house of inheritance is ruled by the Moon representing her royal family who handed down her crown.

Saturn's full aspect is the 3rd aspect which is the sextile, it is aspecting the 2nd house which it rules the sign Capricorn therefore, even though it is Saturn it further empowers the 2nd house and its attributes of wealth and money.

And last but not lease, Rahu is aspecting Venus ruler of the 11th house of gains.

Both her Mars and Jupiter are in the nakshatra of Dhanishta which means the richest one, and her Mercury is in Uttara Bhadrapada the nakshatra for wealth but sometimes denotes wealth from inheritance, which her throne was inherited.

Her majesty has Saturn in the mega rich nakshatra Vishakha.

12th h.	1st h.	2nd h.	3rd h.
♇ 26:19 Rev ☊ 16:05 UBh ♓	ASC 03:26 Ash ♈	♀ 15:41 Roh ♂ 24:33 Mrg ♉	☿ 20:17 Pun ☉ 24:52 Pun ♊
11th h. ♅ 20:39 PBh ♒	John D Rockefeller Sr. Sun 07-08-1838 23:55:00 Richford, NY USA Timezone: 5 DST: 0 Latitude: 42N21'20 Longitude: 76W12'04 Ayanamsha : -21:36:06 Lahiri		4th h. ♋
10th h. ♆ 18:02 Shr ☽ 16:26 Shr ♑			5th h. ♃ 22:45 PPh ♌
9th h. ♐	8th h. ♄℞ 00:49 Vis ♏	7th h. ♎	6th h. ☋ 16:05 Has ♍

John D. Rockefeller was an American industrialist and founder of Standard Oil Enterprise; he was the first to make his fortune through the oil business. He was the son of a poverty ridden con artist. He was an extremely shrewd business man forcing competitors out of business. He married and had five children. By the time of his retirement in 1902 his fortune was worth over 1 billion dollars to which he left the majority of to his oldest son, John D. Jr. before his death.

He has a powerful 2nd house with Venus and Mars there. Venus rules the 2nd house (Taurus) and is situated in the 2nd house, it is the ruler of the house and resides in it. When Venus is in its sign of rulership, either Taurus or Libra or its sign of exaltation, it denotes great wealth and luxuries. Mr. Rockefeller was the richest man in the world and actually the richest man ever if you look at the relative cost of things in his day. Together in the 2nd house he has the all powerful Venus with Mars. Mars rules his 1st house (Aries) which means the ruler of the 1st house is with the ruler of the 2nd house of money in the 2nd house will most definitely brings the money to him. Mars aspects the 8th house (ruled by Scorpio) by opposition and since Mars rules Scorpio it empowers it for what the 8th house is good for, which is the ability to acquire money through others. But since Saturn is there in Scorpio these 2 planets aspecting each other creates a type of persistence that will over ride any opponent. Saturn rules the 11th house of great gains and aspects both Venus and Mars in the 2nd house, so this connects the 11th house ruler with Mars ruler of the 1st (money brought to him) and most importantly the ruler of the 11th house is aspecting the ruler of the 2nd house. Remember, the most powerful influence for money in a chart is when the ruler of the 11th house is connected to the ruler of the 2nd house.

Jupiter in his 5th house of intelligence and speculation brings him the ability to wheel and deal great business opportunities. Jupiter aspects the 1st and 9th house but the sign on the 9th house is Sagittarius which empowers the 9th house for what the 9th house promises which is luck and fortune.

The Lunar Nodes, Rahu and Ketu are aspecting planets for expansion and magnification for these planets to create money in a chart. Rahu is aspecting Saturn which is again the grand ruler of the 11th house of gains, magnifying this ability for gains. Ketu aspects the Moon in the 10th house and also aspects Venus and Mars in the 2nd house. Traditionally Ketu is not perceived as magnifying money but it will cause extremes in some way and because we are activating planets in earth signs in earth houses (artha) we have a connecting force that brings forth great wealth. The Moon in the 10th house of public recognition produces fame and notoriety in a life. One final note, since he did make his fortune through oil notice he has Neptune, the planet ruling oil, in his 10th house of career tightly conjunct his Moon.

The nakshatra Jupiter is in is Purva Phalguni one of the major nakshatras noted for money in a chart. And Rahu is in the nakshatra Uttara Bhadrapada which is another nakshatra noted for financial gains.

John D. Rockefeller has his Saturn in the mega rich nakshatra Vishakha.

6th h. ♇ 21:27 Rev ♓	7th h. ♈	8th h. ☊ 07:40 Kri ♉	9th h. ♃℞ 23:34 Pun ♊
5th h. ♅ 05:12 Dha ♒	Andrew Carnegie Wed 11-25-1835 06:00:00 Dunfermline, Borders Scotland Timezone: 0 DST: 0 Latitude: 56N04'00 Longitude: 03W29'00 Ayanamsha : -21:33:41 Lahiri		10th h. ♋
4th h. ☽ 16:56 Shr ♆ 09:57 USh ♑			11th h. ♌
3rd h. ♐	2nd h. ☋ 07:40 Anu ☉ 10:44 Anu ♂ 17:34 Jye ♀ 23:37 Jye ♏	1st h. ♄ 08:42 Swa Asc 17:55 Swa ☿ 20:54 Vis ♎	12th h. ♍

Andrew Carnegie was a Scottish industrialist who made his fortune through the steel industry. He merged two corporations to form the biggest corporation in the world ever, U. S. Steel Co. He married once and had one daughter.

He was a philanthropist donating around 350 million dollars. His quest for education and knowledge initiated the opening of Public Libraries in the U.S.

His 2nd house of money is empowered by four major planets, which have produced this great fortune. Mars is here in its own sign Scorpio magnificently empowering this house and it is with the planet of luxuries, Venus which rules the 1st house meaning the money is brought to him. Also, in this combination the Sun rules the 11th house of great gains. The most important requirements for wealth are here where both the 2nd house ruler is with the 11th house ruler and they both conjoin the 1st house ruler, All of which means this great fortune is his and all this energy occurs in the house of money, the 2nd house.

The planet of luck, Jupiter is in the 9th house of luck and fortune, and aspects Mercury which rules Gemini the sign ruling the 9th house of luck and fortune that Jupiter occupies. As Jupiter is aspecting the 1st house, this will add positive energy to the 1st house which gives a person confidence and power. Jupiter is also aspecting Saturn in the 1st house, magnifying it with even more power. Saturn is already extraordinarily powerful because it is exalted in the sign of Libra. Jupiter's aspect to Saturn connects the 3 houses that are powerful money houses, the 9th, 1st and the 5th' because Jupiter is in the 9th house, aspecting Saturn in the 1st house and exalted Saturn rules the 5th house (the ultimate intelligence), plus Jupiter is aspecting the 5th house. The 5th house is intelligence and speculation, meaning most great business men have an intuitive edge coupled with a bright and intelligent mind, therefore this is a very important house to have active in making massive fortunes in life.

Rahu is in the 8th house aspecting the Moon, they are both in earth signs indicating the ability to find the resources to make money. As Rahu aspects the Moon this magnifies the Moons power. Rahu in the 8th house of others money gives a wealth of opportunities to work with others with money, plus of course it is aspecting the 2nd house. Ketu the planet that magnifies things as well as Rahu will multiply the ability to expand the power to make money. Particularly because it is next to those 3 enormously powerful planets for money, Mars, Venus and the Sun, tying in the most powerful houses for money, the 2nd, 1st, and the 11th houses.

Andrew Carnegie has four planets plus his ascendant in the mega rich nakshatras, Mercury and his Ascendant are in Vishakha, Saturn is in Swati, and Venus and Mars is in Jyestha.

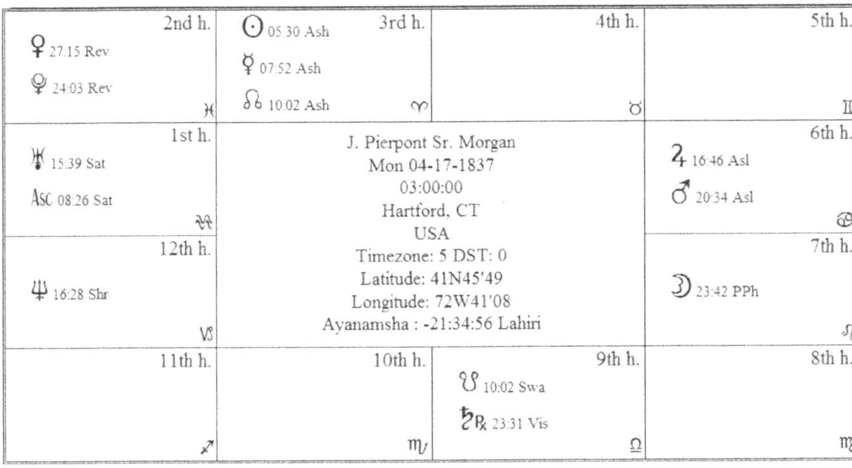

J. P. Morgan was an American financier which founded the J. P. Morgan Co. which amassed one of America's largest fortunes. Since his company had control of most of the business in America he had the most control over the nation at one time. He was credited for the financial success of America. Before the Federal Reserve he saved the United States from bankruptcy single handedly on two occasions.

He was very sickly as a child, and took care of his ill mother. He married twice, his first wife died of tuberculosis and he had 4 children with his second wife.

He loved art, spending more than half his fortune on his personal art collection.

You may have noticed that J.D. Rockefeller, and Andrew Carnegie were born a few years apart, both have exalted Saturn in Libra. They were the true pioneers of business in America.

The most powerful influence in this chart is the exalted Venus in the 2nd house of money. Venus is the most important planet for extravagant wealth. The fact that it is exalted in Pisces and most importantly it is the exact degree of exaltation (27 degrees of Pisces) empowers it all the more. Jupiter the other planet for wealth is aspectin+g Venus making it even more powerful, plus Jupiter is aspecting the 2nd house, ruled by Pisces. Which means it is aspecting the sign it rules, amplifying this house even more to produce what it is good for, which is money. Jupiter is also exalted as well, making it as powerful as possible and it rules Sagittarius the sign on the 11th house of great gains. Therefore, empowering the 11th house for what it is good for, which is exalted gains. With Jupiter's aspect to the 2nd house and it rules the 11th house this connects the 2nd and the 11th houses. This is one of the most powerful determinates of wealth in a chart.

What is most amazing is that both planets that are indicators for wealth and money, Venus and Jupiter are in their exalted signs. Plus Jupiter rules both wealth producing houses the 2nd and 11th houses.

Saturn rules his chart (rules the 1st house) and it is also exalted in the sign of Libra, and is placed in the 9th house of luck and fortune. It is magnified by being conjunct Ketu in the 9th house. Saturn which is ruler of the 1st house aspects by opposition 3 planets in the 3rd house, Rahu, Mercury and the Sun. Saturn's aspect to Mercury connects the 1st house to the 5th house because Mercury rules the fifth house (Gemini). Furthermore, the fact that Mercury is conjunct Rahu expands the mind and intelligence of this individual.

Jupiter is not in an earth sign, actually there are no earth signs in this chart but it is in an earth house, the 6th house (earth houses are 2, 6, and 10 and deal with worldly matters).

The Sun is also in its exaltation sign of Aries giving him great personal power, and it is even magnified with Rahu.

He has four planets in exaltation, Jupiter, Venus, Saturn and the Sun. This emphasizes his power and control in life.

The nakshatras for money are here too, Dhanishta is the nakshatra of his ascendant (degree of his 1st house), and his Moon is in the nakshatra Purva Phalguni and Venus is in Revati.

J. P. Morgan has the mega wealthy nakshatras, Ketu in Swati and Saturn in Vishakha.

One last note, J.P. Morgan had the utmost respect for astrology. He is quoted as saying "Anyone can be a millionaire but to be a billionaire you need an astrologer". His astrologer Evangeline Adams advised him not go on the Titanic, in which he followed this advice.

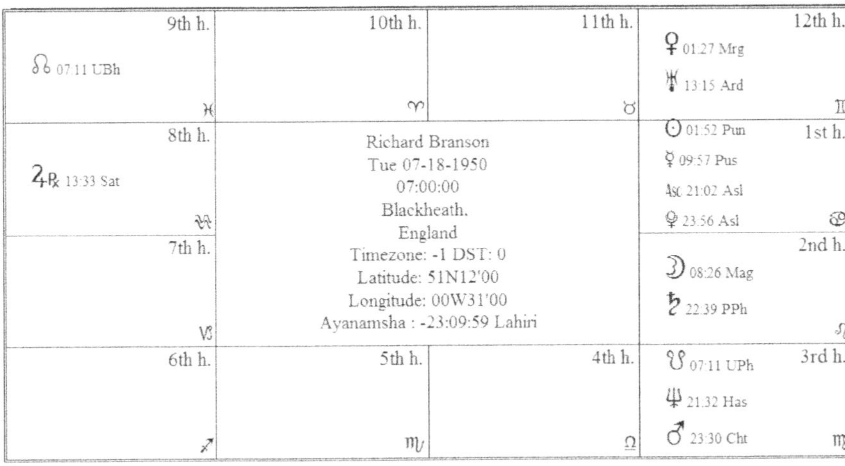

Richard Branson is a British entrepreneur who made his millions on publishing and went on to open both Virgin records and Virgin Atlantic Airways. He then later was successful with film, video and property markets. He began his career when he was only 20 with a student magazine that soon expanded with 40 employees. Only 12 years later he had an empire of 50 companies. He was born for success!

Richard has both the Moon and Saturn in the 2nd house of money, and the Moon rules his 1st house (Cancer) indicating the money comes to him. This is so important that the 1st house ruler be connected to the 2nd house of money. Jupiter aspects both these planets empowering and expanding their capability to produce money all the more. Jupiter rules the 9th house (Pisces) and is in the 8th house of money from others. The real power for this to increase the luck and fortune of an individual is through the connection of Jupiter as ruler of the 9th house aspecting the 2nd house and the planets in the 2nd house (Moon and Saturn). Saturn rules (Aquarius) the 8th house and aspects this house, benefiting his ability to acquire money from others such as investors.

One of the most important rules emphasized in charts of money is the connection of the 2nd house and the 11th house. Here Jupiter aspects Venus (5th aspect) in the 12th house. Venus rules the 11th house and Jupiter aspects the 2nd house and Venus. Therefore, there is a connection of the 2nd and 11th houses through expansive money producing Jupiter.

Venus is the only planet that will prosper in the 12th house and actually indicates wealth when it is in the 12th house.

Rahu has the power to expand things and its placement in the 9th house of fortune will increase riches. Rahu aspects the 5th and 1st houses pertaining to wealth through the mind (5th house) and the 1st house plus it aspects the planets in the 1st house, Sun, Mercury and Pluto. Specifically the Sun rules the 2nd house so Rahu's aspect (5th) will expand the Sun and the house it rules which is the 2nd house of money.

Richard Branson's Rahu is in the wealthy nakshatra Uttara Bhadrapada and his Saturn is in Purva Phalguni.

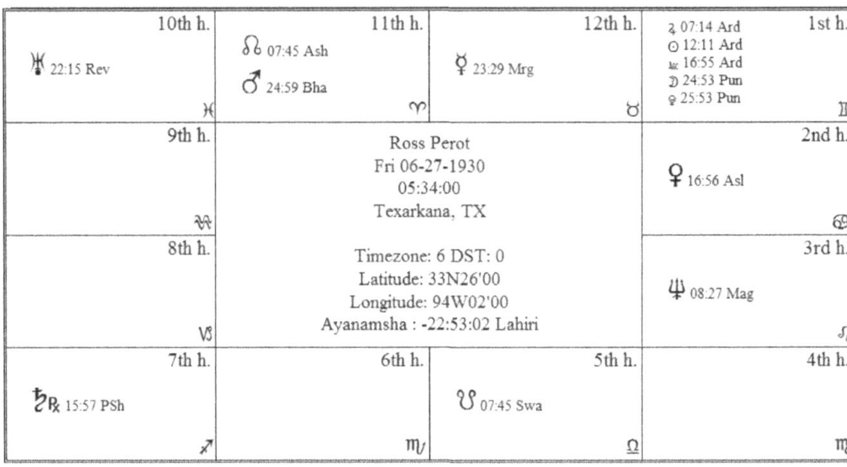

Ross Perot a Texas billionaire built his fortune on high tech, computer, bio-tech and the aero space fields. His multi-million dollar company Electronic Data Systems (EDS) was built on his powerful business ethic. When he sold his company to General Motors it was worth 12 billion dollars. He is noted for his heroic act where he personally rescued two of his employees from Iran after the Ayatollah took over, against diplomatic law. He ran for President of the United States as the Reform Party, using his own money. He created a definite curve ball in the elections. He is a family man married once with five children.

There is a connection of the 2nd and 1st house as one of the most powerful connections for money. The Moon rules the 2nd house (Cancer) and it is in the 1st house. Jupiter the planet of wealth and fortune is in the 1st house adding more benefit to the Moon. Venus the planet of opulent wealth is in the 2nd house of money and it rules the 5th house of intelligence and speculation. Jupiter also aspects the 5th house (speculation) and the 9th house of luck and fortune.

All the 1st house planets, Jupiter, Sun, Moon and Pluto aspect the 7th house and Saturn which rules the 8th and 9th house. Here is a connection of the 1st house to the 9th house (Jupiter in the 1st aspects Saturn ruler of the 9th house). When Jupiter aspects any planet it multiplies its good effects, which it multiplies luck and fortune. Saturn is in Sagittarius which means Jupiter is aspecting the sign it rules empowering this house (7th house) for what it rules, which is strong partnerships. He was married once and has strong business partners. Saturn aspects the 9th house by its 3rd aspect and it rules the 9th enforcing the power of the lucky 9th house.

But the best wealth expanding aspect of this chart is Mars in the 11th house of great gains. Mars here is in its own sign of rulership. Meaning it is the ruler of the 11th house and it is in the 11th house. This extraordinary placement for wealth is also conjunct Rahu which magnifies it all the more. This is an exceptional example for huge wealth. Mars additionally aspects the 2nd house with its 4th aspect therefore, connecting the 11th house with the 2nd house another one of the major requirements for great wealth and money. Mars also aspects the 2nd (4th aspect) and 6th house (8th aspect) and these are the earth or artha houses for worldly matters. Mars is aspecting the 6th house which it rules (Scorpio) which gives him his powerful work ethic.

Rahu the planet of expansion aspects Saturn, the ruler of the 9th house, multiplying his abilities to create more luck and fortune. Ketu in the 5th house aspects (5th aspect) all the 1st house planets, but particularly it aspects Jupiter to the exact degree. This expands Jupiter and Jupiter mutually aspects Ketu empowering it for good.

Ross Perot has the mega rich nakshatra, Ketu is in Swati.

<table>
<tr><td>5th h.
♄ Rx 18:47 Rev
♓</td><td>6th h.
♅ 22:21 Bha
☋ 24:48 Bha
♈</td><td>7th h.
♉</td><td>8th h.
♊</td></tr>
<tr><td>4th h.
♃ 00:59 Dha
♒</td><td colspan="2" rowspan="2">Ted Turner
Sat 11-19-1938
08:50:00
Cincinnati, OH
USA
Timezone: 5 DST: 0
Latitude: 39N09'43
Longitude: 84W27'25
Ayanamsha : -23:00:24 Lahiri</td><td>9th h.
♀ 08:26 Pus
♋</td></tr>
<tr><td>3rd h.
♑</td><td>10th h.
♆ 29:57 UPh
♌</td></tr>
<tr><td>2nd h.
♐</td><td>1st h.
☉ 03:34 Anu
♇ Rx 04:41 Anu
Asc 19:50 Jye
☿ 24:25 Jye
♏</td><td>12th h.
☽ 05:02 Cht
☊ 24:48 Vis
♎</td><td>11th h.
♂ 22:56 Has
♍</td></tr>
</table>

Ted Turner is one of the wealthiest entrepreneurs in America. His fortune is worth around 7 billion. His businesses include Turner Broadcasting, CNN, 2 sports teams and some of MGM. Growing up his father was extremely hard on him, and a memory that haunts him is the suicide of his father at age 53. Then his only sister died of Lupus.

He was called "Ted the Terrible" around his business for his was unyielding and hot temper. He had several marriages before he married actress Jane Fonda. They were married for 10 years, 1991-2001. He is a politically oriented philanthropist and donated 1 billion dollars to the U.N.

The ruler of the 1st house is in the 11th house, connecting the house that represents him (1st house) to the house of great gains (11th house). Mars in the 11th house aspects (4th aspect) the 2nd house of money, connecting the 11th house to the 2nd house, one of the most important features for wealth and money. Mars also aspects the 6th house and Ketu (8th aspect) and Mars rules the 6th house empowering this house for good which is an artha or earth house, pertaining to materialistic matters.

Mercury is in the 1st house and rules the 11th house (Virgo) connecting the house of gains to the 1st house. This is another combination bringing wealth to the person. Actually, Mars and Mercury exchange signs. Mars is in Virgo which is ruled by Mercury and Mercury is in Scorpio ruled by Mars. This links these two planets in a special way.

Mars aspects the 5th house and Saturn by opposition. Generally, whenever Saturn and Mars mutually aspect each other, this aspect generates persistence and drive that great creates success, but with unpleasant characteristics.

Jupiter the planet of expansion and luck aspects the Moon (9th aspect) which rules the 9th house of luck and fortune. This will massively expand the Moon and the house it rules. Jupiter itself becomes powerful here because Rahu is aspecting Jupiter, and Jupiter mutually aspects Rahu. Furthermore, Jupiter is not the only planet to aspect the Moon, for it is conjunct Rahu expanding it all the more.

The Moon rules the 9th house and is in the 12th house of loss with obsessive Rahu causing the loss of his father in a violent manner.

The nakshatras noted for money are here too. Ted Turner has 2 planets plus his Ascendant in the mega rich nakshatras, Rahu is in Vishakha, and his ascendant and Mercury are in Jyeshta. He also has Saturn in Revati and Jupiter in Dhanishta.

11th h.	12th h.	1st h.	2nd h.
☊ 00:52 PBh ♓	♈	Asc 02:32 Kri ♉	♅ 15:01 Ard ♊
10th h. ♃ 08:09 Sat ♒	Christina Onassis Mon 12-11-1950 15:00:00 New York, NY New York USA Timezone: 5 DST: 0 Latitude: 40N42'51 Longitude: 74W00'23 Ayanamsha : -23:10:20 Lahiri		3rd h. ♇ 26:35 Asl ♋
9th h. ♂ 04:03 USh ☽ 00:24 USh ♑			4th h. ♌
8th h. ☿ 15:57 PSh ♀ 02:51 Mul ♐	7th h. ☉ 26:02 Jye ♏	6th h. ♎	5th h. ☋ 00:52 UPh ♄ 08:19 UPh ♆ 25:54 Cht ♍

Christina Onassis was the heiress of her father's shipping industry in Greece which made her one of the richest women in the world. She inherited about a billion dollars of which about 25 million was given to her father's widow, Jackie Onassis Kennedy.

Outwardly, she was very unhappy, looking for love but attracted those only interested in her money, ending in four failed marriages. Her only daughter, Athina acquired her fortune when she died prematurely at age 37. She was overweight and abused her body by constant diets and overeating. Her daughter was only 3 years old when she died.

As expected, her 8th house of money through inheritance is empowered by planets Venus and Mercury. Mercury rules her 2nd house of money and Venus rules her 1st house (Taurus). This combination means her money came to her through the 8th house of inheritance. The ruler of the 1st with the ruler of the 2nd house brings the money to the individual. Furthermore, planets in the 8th house always aspect the 2nd house of money by opposition, and Mercury empowers this house by the fact that Mercury rules the 2nd house (Virgo) and aspects it. Plus Venus as ruler of the 1st house also aspects the 2nd house making this strong connection of the 1st and 2nd house.

Mars is powerful by sign, for Capricorn is the exaltation sign for Mars. It is in the 9th house of luck, fortune and her father from whom her mass fortune was inherited.

Saturn as ruler of the 9th house of fortune is aspecting the 11th house by opposition, which connects the 5th house of intelligence to the 11th house of gains. Rahu is also in this house expanding it more for great gains.

Jupiter, ruler of the 11th house, is in the 10th house which aspects the earth houses the 2nd and 6th houses which pertain to materialistic pursuits. The connection for the 11th house and 2nd house is here with Jupiter because it rules the 11th house (Pisces) and aspects the 2nd house (5th aspect).

Christina Onassis has her Sun in the mega rich nakshatra Jyestha.

<table>
<tr><td>4th h.
♓</td><td>5th h.
♈</td><td>6th h.
♃℞ 23:26 Mrg
♉</td><td>7th h.
♅ 27:05 Pun
♊</td></tr>
<tr><td>3rd h.
♒</td><td colspan="2" rowspan="2">Oprah Winfrey
Fri 01-29-1954
04:15:00
Kosciusko, MS Mississippi
USA
Timezone: 6 DST: 0
Latitude: 33N03'27
Longitude: 89W35'15
Ayanamsha : -23:13:13 Lahiri</td><td>8th h.
☋ 00:42 Pun
♋</td></tr>
<tr><td>2nd h.
☿ 25:55 Dha
☉ 15:45 Shr
♀ 15:37 Shr
☊ 00:42 USh
♑</td><td>9th h.
♇ 00:55 Mag
♌</td></tr>
<tr><td>1st h.
Asc 03:03 Mul
♐</td><td>12th h.
♂ 00:21 Vis
☽ 11:10 Anu
♏</td><td>11th h.
♆ 02:50 Cht
♄ 15:49 Swa
♎</td><td>10th h.
♍</td></tr>
</table>

Oprah Winfrey has the most amazing chart for wealth and fortune! She made her fortune through acting and mass media. Inventing herself through insightful informative talk shows that dominated the networks. Her business sense made her the ultimate success and one of the richest women in the world, with her company Harpo Communications. Oprah made it all on her own with all odds against her, being a black woman from Mississippi without a mother. Oprah is a workaholic, never taking time out to have a family or marriage.

The ruler of the 2nd house, Saturn is exalted in Libra in the 11th house. The connection of 2nd house to the 11th is the most powerful connection for wealth and money, but additionally this planet Saturn is exalted, which magnifies this all the more. Furthermore, the ruler of the 11th house is Venus and it is in the 2nd house, another connection of the house of money (2nd house) to the house of great gains (11th house). Actually, this is a really strong connection for both Saturn and Venus are in each other's sign of rulership. Venus is in Capricorn ruled by Saturn and Saturn is in Libra ruled by Venus. This is called mutual reception (parivartana yoga) and when this occurs with the 2nd and 11th house rulers you are assured great wealth.

Venus in the 2nd house is conjunct Rahu, which magnifies Venus the planet of opulent riches even more. When you think it can't get better, it does, because

Venus is exactly conjunct the Sun ruler of the 9th house of luck and fortune. Please note, this is no ordinary conjunction because when planets get too close to the Sun they can have a negative effect for the Sun bums up the other planets, this is called combustion. But in this case it is the exact same degree which is rare, and is called cazimi which means Venus is not hurt by the Sun and becomes more powerful because it unites as one with the Sun, making them a giant dynamo!

On top of all this power, fortune, luck, and opulent money all the planets in the 2nd house, Venus, Rahu, Sun, and Mercury are all aspected by Jupiter (9th aspect), adding more expansion and multiplying the wealth even more. Jupiter's aspect to the 2nd house planets connects it to the 2nd house plus the houses these planets rule, Venus the 11th house, the Sun the 9th house and because Jupiter rules the 1st house (ruler of the chart) this means the wealth is brought to her through this connection.

Jupiter also aspects Mars ruler of the 5th house (intelligence and speculation) and the Moon by opposition, and the Moon rules the 8th house of money through others, which is probably how she got her start.

Jupiter is in an earth sign and an earth house and aspects all 4 planets in the 2nd house which are also in an earth/artha house and sign. The earth signs are 2, 6 and 10 and the earth signs are Taurus, Virgo, and Capricorn. This means earthly materialistic things are bestowed onto this individual.

The nakshatra for wealth in Oprah's chart is Mercury which is in Dhanishta, which means the richest one. Oprah Winfrey's powerful mega rich nakshatras are Saturn in Swati and Mars is in Vishakha.

4th h. ♃ 22:41 Rev ♓	5th h. ☊ 14:49 Bha ♈	6th h. ♇ 16:11 Roh ♆ 17:08 Roh ♉	7th h. ♊
3rd h. ♂ 29:39 PBh ♒	J. Paul Getty Thu 12-15-1892 08:43:00 Minneapolis, MN Minnesota USA		8th h. ♋
2nd h. ♑	Timezone: 6 DST: 0 Latitude: 44N58'48 Longitude: 93W15'49 Ayanamsha : -22:21:33 Lahiri		9th h. ♌
1st h. Asc 13:47 PSh ☉ 01:47 Mul ♐	12th h. ☿℞ 23:53 Jye ♏	11th h. ☋ 14:49 Swa ♅ 16:48 Swa ☽ 21:03 Vis ♀ 28:43 Vis ♎	10th h. ♄ 19:15 Has ♍

John Paul Getty was the richest man in the world when he struck oil in the Middle East in 1953. He was an American entrepreneur in both real estate and oil. He came from an affluent family, for his father was in the oil business and gave him his start in the Oklahoma oil fields. He inherited 15 million dollars from his father when he died and multiplied this money amassing an estate worth four billion dollars. He was known for being extremely cheap with his money. When his grandson was kidnapped he refused to pay the ransom, but after the gangsters cut off the child's ear and sent it to them he lent the money for the ransom to his son with interest.

His 11th house has Venus in Libra one of the most powerful signs for wealth. Venus is the most powerful planet for extremes in wealth and when it is in one of the power signs (Taurus, Libra and Pisces) and rules the 11th house of great gains you can bet there is a fortune in this individual's life. When one of the natural money planets (Jupiter and Venus) is in the 11th house of gains it automatically aspects the powerful 5th house of intelligence and speculation.

In his 5th house he has Rahu which expands the mind almost to excess but will increase money. Rahu in the 5th house aspects the 1st house and the 9th house, both are houses that need connection for wealth. In his 1st house there is the Sun which rules the 9th house of luck and fortune plus Rahu's aspect expands this all the more.

The ruler of his chart (ruler of the 1st house) is Jupiter, and Jupiter is very strong in the sign it rules, Pisces. Furthermore; Jupiter aspects Saturn by opposition and Saturn rules the 2nd house of money. In this way Jupiter ruler of the chart is connected to the 2nd house ruler, Saturn.

The nakshatra for wealth and is consistently one of the more common nakshatras in charts of wealth is Revati, and his Jupiter is in Revati. John Paul Getty has four planets in the mega rich nakshatras, Venus and the Moon are in Vishakha, Ketu is in Swati and Mercury is in Jyestha.

7th h. ☉ 26:28 Rev ☿℞ 10:26 UBh ♅ 03:57 UBh ♓	8th h. ♈	9th h. ♉	10th h. ♇ 19:47 Ard ☊ 28:27 Pun ♊
6th h. ☽ 20:47 PBh ♀ 10:31 Sat ♒	Hugh Hefner Fri 04-09-1926 16:20:00 Chicago, IL USA Timezone: 6 DST: 0 Latitude: 41N51'00 Longitude: 87W39'00 Ayanamsha : -22:49:22 Lahiri		11th h. ♆ 29:19 Asl ♋
5th h. ♃ 27:51 Dha ♂ 19:59 Shr ♑			12th h. ♌
4th h. ☋ 28:27 USh ♐	3rd h. ♄℞ 02:16 Vis ♏	2nd h. ♎	1st h. Asc 03:03 UPh ♍

Hugh Hefner is an American entrepreneur who made his fortune in publishing, movies, music, and casinos and by the age of 40 he was worth well over 100 million. He began his career with the first publication of "Playboy" magazine in 1953, and by 1960 he opened the first Playboy Club in Chicago. He blames his success on his upbringing. He was raised in a Puritan home where there was no external show of any affection or emotion. He is constantly reinventing himself and projects the life he lives through his magazines.

I wanted to use a chart that has no planets in either the 2nd or 11th house, so upon first glance wealth and money don't pop out. For these 2 houses are the very houses that mean MONEY! But notice that both the ruler of the 2nd house and the 11th house, Venus rules the 2nd house (Libra) and the Moon rules the 11th house (Cancer) are conjunct in the 6th house. So, both of these houses are connected. Additionally, Venus also rules the 9th house of luck and fortune. Venus for a Virgo ascendant is the money and luck planet since it rules the 2nd house of money and the 9th house of luck and fortune. Since it is with the Moon, ruler of the 11th house of gains, it really empowers the 11th house to produce its power for gains.

Jupiter the other fortunate planet for money is in the 5th house of intelligence with Mars. Jupiter is weak by sign, Jupiter is debilitated in Capricorn, but by the fact that it is with Mars, in its exaltation sign of Capricorn, it is uplifted by the strength of Mars. Any time a planet is debilitated but is conjunct an exalted planet it gives the debilitated planet strength. Since they are both in the sign Capricorn, which is ruled by Saturn and Saturn aspects (3rd aspect) the 5th house then Saturn empowers the 5th house for what it indicates, which is great luck with speculation and intelligence. Jupiter also aspects the 9th and 1st house (5th and 9th aspects) connecting it to these houses of wealth and they are in the earth signs of worldly matters. Here is a connection to all the important houses for money, wealth, speculation, intelligence, luck and fortune and great gains (2nd, 5th, 9th and 11th houses and the 1st house). Jupiter's aspect to the 1st brings the luck to him. Rahu the other planet that expands what it aspects is in the 10th house aspecting the 2nd house of money, Venus and the Moon which are the rulers of both the money houses 2nd and 11th.

Mercury ruler of the 1st house (Virgo) aspects the 1st house by opposition and rules the 1st house, so it does empower the 1st house. This is really fortunate because Mercury is weak by being in its debilitation sign, but does enhance the 1st house.

Hough Hefner has his Saturn in the mega rich nakshatra Vishakha. He also has 3 of the money producing nakshatras, Jupiter in Dhanishta, Mercury in Uttara Bhadrapada, and the Sun in Revati.

12th h. ♆ 12:52 UBh ♓	1st h. ☉ 16:46 Bha ♇ 18:51 Bha ☿ 26:54 Kri Asc 29:14 Kri ♈	2nd h. ☋ 15:18 Roh ♀ 19:48 Roh ♅ 26:25 Mrg ♉	3rd h. ♂ 09:01 Ard ♊
11th h. ♒	William Randolf Hearst Wed 04-29-1863 05:58:00 San Francisco, CA USA Timezone: 8 DST: 0 Latitude: 37N46'30 Longitude: 122W25'06 Ayanamsha : -21:57:09 Lahiri		4th h. ♋
10th h. ♑			5th h. ☽ 25:37 PPh ♌
9th h. ♐	8th h. ☊ 15:18 Anu ♏	7th h. ♎	6th h. ♄℞ 07:38 UPh ♃℞ 28:27 Cht ♍

William Randolph Hearst was an American industrialist founder of the Hearst chains of publications. He made it big with his sensationalism in his newspapers. He later expanded into films and radio. In his prime he was one of the richest men of his day. His father a Senator gave him his start with the San Francisco Examiner, and by 1937 he owned 37 publications. He is most noted for the mansion he built called San Simeon. It was a Mediterranean style City on a hill. It was the most extravagant mansion built at that time.

He has one of the most powerful indicators of wealth with Venus in Taurus. Venus is all powerful to produce grand riches and luxuries when is it at its peak of strength in the signs Taurus, Libra or Pisces. His Venus in the 2nd house of money, gives great strength to create riches. Additionally, Venus is uplifted more with the aspect of Jupiter (9th aspect). Jupiter multiplies the planets it aspects which is Venus ruler of the 2nd house, in the 2nd house. Specifically, when a planet is in its own sign of rulership (Venus rules Taurus) and it is with Ketu it will always magnify the house and produce on a grand scale what that house rules, and in this case the 2nd house rules money. Ordinarily, Ketu depletes and causes a vacuum for the house it resides. But this specific rule changesKetu qualities to instead magnify instead of deplete a house and the areas that house rules.

Jupiter is conjunct Saturn in the 6th house of work and Saturn rules (Aquarius) the 11th house of great gains. Jupiter aspects both the ruler of the 2nd house of money (Venus) and the ruler 11th house of great gains (Saturn). Therefore, Jupiter connects the 2 houses of money (houses 2 and 11).

Mars is in the 3rd house of communications and aspects (4th aspect) Jupiter ruler of the 9th house of publications. Both Mars and Jupiter are in a Mercury ruled sign (Mars in Gemini and Jupiter in Virgo) this indicates wealth through the field of communication, in which his newspaper publications was his goldmine.

William Randolph Hearst's Moon is in the money producing nakshatra Purva Phalguni.

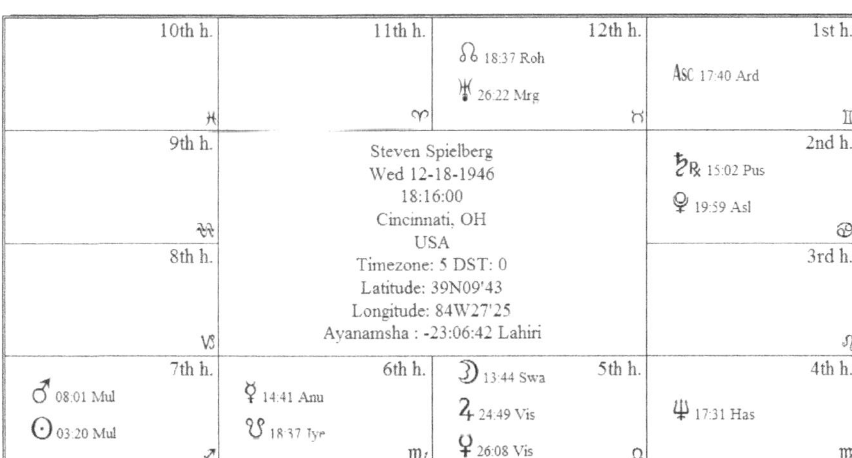

Steven Spielberg is an iconic movie producer and director. Winner of the academy award for best picture, Schindler's List and an Oscar for Saving Private Ryan. His lists of movies entail many of those that shape a generation. He is pure genius with incredible talent. Growing up he felt like an outcast due to his parents constantly moving and being the only Jewish kid in the class. It is no wonder he immersed himself into his creative ability, working with film at an early age.

Actually, the 5th house is the house of talent, creative ability and in terms of money it is the house of speculation and intelligence. In this most wonderful house Spielberg has the 2 natural money planets both Venus and Jupiter. The signs that Venus is the most powerful for wealth are Taurus, Libra and Pisces in which has been a common denominator in many of these wealth producing charts of the mega rich. He has Venus in Libra which is in the house of talent and intelligence (5th house) which Venus also has rulership over this blessed house. Additionally, Venus is magnified by the aspect of the conjunction of Jupiter in this house. Next to both Jupiter and Venus is the Moon which rules the 2nd house of money. So here we have the 5th house ruler with the 2nd house ruler in the powerful 5th house both conjunct Jupiter expanding their power all the more. The planets in the 5th Jupiter, Venus and the Moon also aspects the 11th house by opposition. Remember any planets in the 5th house always aspect the 11th house which is powerful for wealth and great gains. The Moon ruler of the 2nd house is conjunct both natural benefics for wealth in the 5th house of creativity and aspects the 11th house of gains.

Saturn is in the 2nd house of money and rules the 9th house of luck and fortune. Jupiter in the 5th house aspects the 9th house of luck and fortune and the 1st house expanding these houses and his ability to produce wealth.

The most powerful connection for wealth is the 2nd house connected to the 11th house. The way in which the 11th house is connected to the 2nd house (houses for money) is the fact that Mars as ruler of the 11th house (Aries) aspects the 2nd house (8th aspect). And the Moon ruler of the 2nd house aspects the 11th house by opposition.

Steven Spielberg has four planets in the ultra rich nakshatras, his Venus and Jupiter are in Vishakha, Moon in Swati and Ketu in Jyestha.

Donald Trump came from a very affluent family. His father gave him his start in the business world of Real Estate. Donald went on to be one of New York Cities premiere owners of the most expensive Real Estate in the world. He prides himself in buying losing property and bringing it back. He is known for having many extreme ups and downs, claiming bankruptcy, and then making a complete come back. He was a star on his own television show "The Apprentice", he loves being in the public eye. He has married three times to beautiful successful women. His net worth is around 3 billion dollars. In 2016 he became the 45 President of the United States.

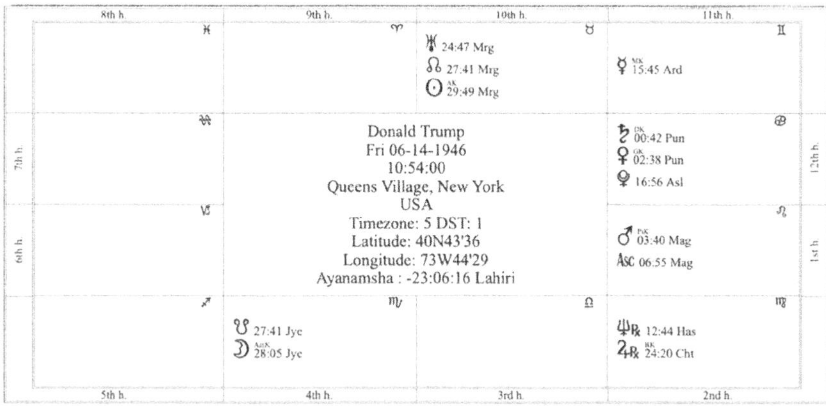

Trump has a Leo Ascendant that sits exactly on the fixed star Regulus, which is the heart of the lion and represents powerful leaders. The chart ruler is the Sun (ruling the ascendant) and is in the 10th house of career and purpose. The Sun is with Rahu expanding his sense of power and ego. The Sun with Rahu in the 10th house is a raja yoga as the Sun rules a trikona and sits in the 10th house, a kendra (angle). Uranus with the Sun and Rahu indicate unpredictable outcomes. Plus, Jupiter aspects his Sun, Rahu and Uranus expanding his potential even more.

Mars is the planet for real-estate, and it is conjunct the ascendant in the sign of Leo. It's ruler the Sun is in the 10th house of career.

Jupiter is in the 2nd house of earned money increasing his ability for the acquisition for wealth and money. One of the most significant indicators for money is when the 2nd house is connected to the 11th house. Here his 2nd house ruling planet Mercury is in the 11th house in its own sign of rulership, Gemini. Mercury in the 11th house, ruling the 11th house of great gains is incredibly powerful for wealth and money.

Notice that Sun and Moon are in opposition with Rahu and Ketu, which means he was born on a full Moon, but this full Moon is also a Lunar eclipse because it is with the lunar nodes, meaning his life is destined for extremes and greatness.

Donald Trump has his Moon and Ketu in the ultra-rich nakshatra Jyestha.

The next 3 charts of Michael Milken, President George W. Bush and Sylvester Stallone are interesting because they are similar to Donald Trump's chart. All were born in the same time period. Notice the similarities in the charts and the close time frame that these four individuals were born. They were all destined to be leaders and have the intelligence and advantage to be wealthy and rich. They all have the Kala Sarpa yoga where all the planets are on one side of Rahu and Ketu. This indicates major highs and lows in a lifetime. An interesting characteristic of the Kala Sarpa yoga is the after incredible lows the individual usually achieves an incredible high that surpasses anything achieved before. All these individuals have had this experience.

9th h. ♓	10th h. ♈	11th h. ♅ 25:56 Mrg ☊ 27:29 Mrg ♉	12th h. ☉ 18:55 Ard ♊
8th h. ♒	Michael Milken Thu 07-04-1946 07:31:00 Los Angeles, CA USA Timezone: 8 DST: 0 Latitude: 34N03'08 Longitude: 118W14'34 Ayanamsha : -23:06:20 Lahiri		1st h. ♄ 03:10 Pun ☿ 14:57 Pus ♇ 17:25 Asl Asc 22:18 Asl ♀ 26:15 Asl ♋
7th h. ♑			2nd h. ♂ 15:07 PPh ♌
6th h. ♐	5th h. ☋ 27:29 Jye ♏	4th h. ♎	3rd h. ☽ 00:34 UPh ♆ 12:48 Has ♃ 24:55 Cht ♍

Michael Milken is an American stockbroker who made a fortune, $550 million in 1987, through insider trading for junk bonds. In 1989, he was indicted on 98 counts of racketeering and securities fraud. In April 1990 he pleaded guilty to six felonies, including illegally concealing stock positions, helping clients evade income taxes, and a conspiracy involving secret record keeping with stock speculator Ivan Boesky. His financial losses totaled $1.1 billion in fines and restitution.

His interest in adult and children's education formulated his "Knowledge Universe" which had sales of more than $1 billion in 1997. He made back his billion dollars! If you have the great ability to make money, you never lose it. You can always make it back.

Mars is ruler of the 5th house of intelligence and creativity and resides in the 2nd house of wealth and money. Rahu and Ketu reside in both the 11th house and 5th giving power and money with Rahu in the 11th house. Rahu aspects Jupiter, and Jupiter aspects Rahu in the 11th house. This is expansive for the 11th house of great gains. Jupiter with Neptune and the Moon in the 3rd house give him talents and abilities to be creative.

Ketu in the 5th house aspects the planets in the 1st house connecting Venus the ruler of the 11th house of gains. He has an incredible mind that enables him to make back all the money he lost in a very short time. The ruler of the 2nd house, the Sun does seem to be a bit disconnected to the other planets. This can be indicative of his imprisonment for his corrupt dealings with the junk bonds for the 12th house rules prisons.

charts, Jyeshta.

<table>
<tr><td>9th h.
♓</td><td>10th h.
♈</td><td>11th h.
♅ 26:02 Mrg
☊ 27:28 Mrg
♉</td><td>12th h.
☉ 20:40 Pun
♊</td></tr>
<tr><td>8th h.
♒</td><td colspan="2" rowspan="2">GEORGE BUSH JR
Sat 07-06-1946
07:26:00
NEW HAVEN, CT
USA
Timezone: 5 DST: 1
Latitude: 41N18'29
Longitude: 72W55'43
Ayanamsha : -23:06:20 Lahiri</td><td>1st h.
♄ 03:23 Pus
As 14:00 Pus
☿ 16:43 Asl
♇ 17:28 Asl
♀ 28:23 Asl
♋</td></tr>
<tr><td>7th h.
♑</td><td>2nd h.
♂ 16:12 PPh
♌</td></tr>
<tr><td>6th h.
♐</td><td>5th h.
☋ 27:28 Jye
♏</td><td>4th h.
♎</td><td>3rd h.
♆ 12:49 Has
☽ 23:36 Cht
♃ 25:02 Cht
♍</td></tr>
</table>

George Bush Jr. became the 43rd President of the United States of America in the year 2000. At first glance, his chart compares to Michael Milken's amazingly, for there is little difference. President Bush was born two days later but around the same time, giving them both the same sign on the ascendant. As we delve deeper within these charts we will see how they differ, but they do give overall success with major ups and downs.

This chart is incredibly similar to Micheal Milken's chart. The main difference with just the birth chart is that the Moon is closer to Jupiter, which will make one more refined and spiritually driven. All the wealth producing aspects that were in Micheal Milken's chart are also in President Bush's chart. Additionally, Jupiter does aspect the 9th house by opposition and it rules the sign Pisces on the 9th house, empowering the spiritual qualities of luck and protection Jupiter and the 9th house provide.

The 5th house is also aspected by Mars which rules the 5th house giving deep powers for concentration and intelligence. I know many made fun of this President for giving the impression of being less intelligent but don't let that persona fool you, for he is extremely sharp and highly intelligent. Whenever Mars is associated with the 5th house it denotes high intelligence for Mars rules intelligence and so does the 5th house.

The mutual exchange of the signs of the planets Moon and Mercury will intensify the mental thinking qualities, connecting the power of these individuals for it is connecting the 1st house with the 3rd house. The ability to express themselves through powerful communication skills particularly writing is prominent in these charts.

<table>
<tr><td>4th h.
♓</td><td>5th h.
♈</td><td>6th h.
♅ 26:04 Mrg
☊ 27:29 Mrg
♉</td><td>7th h.
☉ 21:08 Pun
♊</td></tr>
<tr><td>3rd h.
♒</td><td rowspan="2" colspan="2">Sylvester Stallone
Sat 07-06-1946
19:20:00
New York, NY
USA
Timezone: 5 DST: 1
Latitude: 40N42'51
Longitude: 74W00'23
Ayanamsha : -23:06:20 Lahiri</td><td>8th h.
♄ 03:27 Pus
☿ 17:10 Asl
♇ 17:29 Asl
♀ 28:57 Asl
♋</td></tr>
<tr><td>2nd h.
♑</td><td>9th h.
♂ 16:29 PPh
♌</td></tr>
<tr><td>1st h.
Asc 05:26 Mul
♐</td><td>12th h.
☋ 27:29 Jye
♏</td><td>11th h.
♎</td><td>10th h.
♆ 12:50 Has
♃ 25:04 Cht
☽ 29:39 Cht
♍</td></tr>
</table>

Sylvester Stallone is an American actor who made a huge success with his breakthrough movie "Rocky" which was an overnight success. By the mid 1980's he was making 12 million a movie surpassing the greats at that time, Hoffman and Beatty in money per picture. He had a difficult start in life, coming from a broken home and living in the slums of New York City. He was so rebellious that he got kicked out of 14 schools in 11 years.

He has Jupiter and the Moon in conjunction in his 10th house of career. This is extraordinary for success and power with his career. The ruler of his Chart is Sagittarius, therefore Jupiter is his ruler and it resides the 10th house. This means his career is the most important aspect of his life.

Mars rules the 5th house and resides in the 9th house of luck and opportunities. Connections of the 9th and 5th houses are very fortunate and will give one opportunities to express ones talents to the world. His movies gave him the opportunities to tell his imaginative stories through the medium of film.

The most interesting thing of his chart is the planets in his 8th house which can be very destructive, but when it comes to money the 8th house rules money that comes through others.

The Moon and Mercury exchange signs in all 3 of these charts. This involves the 8th house and the 10th house for Silvester. The 8th house can be a very complicated house with much depth. Many times people with great charisma have important planets here, but they have many trials and tribulations to overcome in this life time.

Looking at this configuration it means he had to get investors to give him the money to achieve his dreams. He was a great success due to the Jupiter/ Moon conjunction in his career house. The Moon in the 10th house often times gives fame.

All four charts have all the planets on one side of the lunar nodes (Rahu and Ketu). This is a specific formation seen in the lives of many who have a definite fate to fulfill in this lifetime. In Vedic astrology it is called Kala Sarpa Yoga.

In these charts (Trump, Milken, Bush, and Stallone) they all have Ketu in the mega, ultra rich nakshatra.

Outline

1) Venus is the planet for huge opulent wealth, and its most powerful placement for wealth is in its sign of rulership or exalted: Taurus, Libra and Pisces.

2) Jupiter is the planet for wealth and money, and when it aspects a house or a planet it will empower and expand its promise.

3) The houses of money are 2nd house: money, 11th house: great money, 5th house: money from intelligence, talent or speculation, 9th house: luck and fortune, 8th house: others money, Inheritance

4) The 2nd house of money and 1st house are connected: it brings the money to the YOU.

5) The 2nd house is connected to the 11th house of great gains.

6) When both the 2nd and the 11th house are mutually connected there is always great wealth.

7) The 5th house of talent is connected to houses 1, 2, 9, or 11.

8) The 9th house of fortune is connected to houses 1, 2, 5 or 11.

9) The 8th house is money from others, such as inheritance, marriage or investors, planets in this house will bring money through others, but the ruler of the 8th house usually brings problems with the money.

10) When a planet aspects a house that it rules (even if there are no planets there) it empowers that house to produce in great amounts what that house is good for, and the area of life the house rules.

11) The earth (artha houses) either by house or sign will promote wealth. Houses: 2nd house, 6th house, and 10th house. The earth signs: Taurus, Virgo, and Capricorn

12) Signs and Nakshatras seen most in mega wealthy people's charts:

    Signs: Libra and Scorpio

    Nakshatras for the ultra mega rich: Jyestha, Vishakha, and Swati

    Other nakshatras that are prominent are Dhanishta, Purva Phalguni, and Revati

The question that will be addressed here is "Can someone who has a chart without all these money combinations change their fate and become prosperous?" My answer to this is "yes" but it takes a shift of consciousness, which is hard. But with work it can be done!

In the following chapters ways to make money through astrology will be explained. Even though you may not have the specified alignments outlined in this chapter, using the transits of the planets you can create a temporary alignment.

Chapter 7
How to Determine Career or Life Purpose

President Theodore Roosevelt kept his horoscope mounted on a chess board in the oval office. When asked about it he would reply, "I always keep my weather eye on the opposition of my seventh house Moon to my first house Mars."

Career or life purpose is extremely important to consider today since most of our time is spent within our work place. In some cultures there is no freedom to choose due to the caste system and there are simply no opportunities. And in other cultures it is still expected that one must continue in the father's business or profession. But in the Western world in the 21st century there are so many choices one is confused as to which direction to head.

Additionally, there are usually changes in careers in a lifetime. As a life changes, so do the career interests and opportunities. Careers that are personally fulfilling using a particular talent the individual possesses usually last the longest. It really depends on a person's personality as to what goals are desired by an individual. Some people may want status while others want financial rewards. Some may enjoy the public and travel while others will need solitude and stability and no travel. All these variables will be addressed here. Usually the attempt to figure one's life profession will reveal all these variables.

The first assessment is the 10th house. It is the house of career and profession. Also the 6th house for work, but it usually has to do with conditions within the workplace. It can be indicative of careers of service or simply jobs to pay the bills, but not a profession. Look at what planets are located in these 2 houses and what these planets are karakas for, as well as the houses they rule. The houses these planets rule located in the career houses (6 and 10) will tell a lot as to what kind of career they will have.

The ascendant and the ruling planet of the ascendant, to which house this planet resides in will be will the main interest of the individual throughout life.

The next step is to see what houses the rulers of the 2 houses of work and career, 6 and 10 occupy. These areas will be of vital importance as to the talents and interests of the individual.

The planets that are the indicators for career are Sun, Mercury, Saturn, and Jupiter, because they are the indicators for the 10th house, the house of Career. Look at the houses they occupy in relation to interest and abilities. The Sun is the planet of leadership and power and is vitally important to career. Mercury is our mental abilities, which play out imperatively with career interest. Saturn as ruler of the 10th sign Capricorn will tell where we are organized and disciplined. Jupiter as the king of the planets gives us clues into our talents.

The 2nd house and its ruler can indicate the way in which we make our money, therefore gives clues to the profession or career. It is the 2nd, 6th, and 10th houses that are the artha houses. Artha is recognition in the material world and wealth, so all three of these houses are indicative of our career choices.

Saturn is the main indicator of career based on the fact that Capricorn is the 10th sign of the natural zodiac, and Saturn rules Capricorn. Saturn used as the ascendant can indicate career choices. This means to take Saturn where it is in the birth chart and make it and the sign it is in the new ascendant. With this the houses all the other planets fall into with the new ascendant using Saturn's sign will give further details about career and purpose.

Signs, Nakshatras, Planets and Houses in Career Choices

Aries: (1st house) military, police, sports, racing, (running, horses, cars, boats etc.) fast travel, pioneers, birth, emergency doctors, emergency medical technicians, ambulance drivers, firefighters

Ashwini- horses, jockeys, fast travel, travel agents, healers, police

Bharani- gynecology (childbirth), death-funeral directors, film and music industry, tobacco, coffee, tea industry, distribution, production, and processing of food

Krittika- protector, law enforcer, food-cook, fire departments, use of fire to make things like a blacksmith, tailors, barbers or beauticians

Taurus: (2nd house) arts, flowers, decorating, music, painter, make up, fashion, perfume, singing, song writer, poet, beef industry, speech therapist, orator, financial advisor, banker, botanist, landscaper

Rohini- fine wines, foods, luxuries, fashion designers, dancing, restaurant and hotel business Mrigashira- searching, forest ranger, collectors, researchers, butchers

Gemini: (3rd house) all communication fields, writers, publishers, teachers, travel, T.V., telephones, computers, good with hands and in building and creating, comedians, good with numbers, astrologers

Ardra- renovation, fixing disasters, writers

Punarvasu- writers, publishers, mystics, spiritual teachers, philosopher, poets

Cancer: (4th house) food service, shelters, mothers, nourishing foods, chefs, beverage services, dairy farms, securities, Medicare, real estate, homes, land, protection

Pushya- dairy operators, professors, nourishing foods, babies, grains

Ashlesha- medicines that heal, pharmacist, homeopathy, hypnotist, psycho-analysis, chemical engineers, drug dealers

Leo: (5th house) politicians, CEOs, Presidents, Kings, artists, advisors, sports, leadership positions, actors, theater, entertainment, stock market traders and analysis, speculations and gambling, astrologers

Magha- heritage, antiques, archeologist, historians, genealogy, forefathers, kings, Presidents, well established universities

Purva Phalguni- actors, musicians, models, radio, television personalities, theater, creative artists, vacations and entertainment, professions connected to marriage, wedding planners

Uttara Phalguni- marriage rituals, wedding planners, social worker, media personalities, sports superstars, philanthropist

Virgo: (6th house) all service professions, nutritionist, dieticians, food service, waiters, chefs, doctors, healers, nurses, flight attendants, restaurants, CPAs, beverage service, health facilities, caretakers, employees, medical professions, councilors, claims adjustors, butlers, maids, working with animals, vets

Hasta- public servants, hand doctors, palmist, artist, craftsman, comedians, magicians , sewing, hand crafts

Chitra- interior design, gemologist, jewelry, architects, the arts, painting

Libra: (7th House) judges, politics, negotiator, mediator, lobbyist, marriage councilors, music, art, fashion, design.

Swati- business skills, can sway both ways, politicians, legal professions, merchants, good salesmen, and talkers

Vishakha- politicians, determination, victories, conquerors

Scorpio: (8th house) tax collectors, CPAs, insurance adjustors, insurance business, morticians, funeral homes, grave sites, drag councilors, psychoanalysis, recovery, researchers, detectives, scientist, private investigation, fraud experts, criminals, mafia, murder lawyers, bill collectors, sex therapist, deep discoveries, mediums, psychics, astrologers, metaphysics

Anuradha- business management, criminal lawyers, organizers of large groups, leaders

Jyeshtha- police detectives, mystics, psychics, military leaders, shamans, those involved in the supernatural

Sagittarius: (9th house) lawyers, philosophers, professors, priest, ministers, political rights activist, missionaries, aviation, pilots, gurus, spokesmen, lecturer, publishing, judges, astrologers, spiritual pilgrimages, long distance travel

Mula- destruction, lawyers, public speakers, writers, spiritual teachers, doctors, medicine especially working with herbs and roots, investigators, researchers, medicine.

Purva Ashadha- writers, teachers, debaters, travel industry, foreign trades, professions associated with water, shipping sailing, water utilities

Capricorn: (10th house) bosses, Waste and water clean up, leadership, fame, government work, economist, headhunters, government agencies and officials, Presidents, leadership

Uttara Ashadha- government jobs, social work, military work, well mannered people, etiquette

Shravana- teachers, speech therapist, councilors, librarians, linguist, news broadcasters, educators

Aquarius: (11th house) humanitarians, group politics, large institutions, inventors, computer programmers, large corporations, jobs where large sums of money come from, organizer, astronomers, astrologers, electricity

Dhanishta- musicians, scientist, research, real estate, charitable organizations

Shatabhishak- astrologers, astronomers, electricians, healers, rocket scientist, nuclear scientist, aircraft

Pisces: (12th house) astronauts, astronomers, aerospace, great imagination and no boundaries, ocean, water, oceanographer, film, photography, gas, oil, prisons, retreats, spas, ashrams, foreign trade, hospitals, resorts, foot doctor-podiatrist

Purva Bhadrapada- administrative planners, black magicians, priests, research skills, fanatics, terrorist, those that deal with death, hospice workers

Uttara Bhadrapada- charitable work, non profit organizations, writers, philosophers, teachers, saints, incredible insights

Revati- film actors, vets, psychics, travel planners, travel agents, foster parents, anything that deals with time, making watches, clocks or calendars

Planets for Career

Sun: Presidents, bosses, and politicians

Moon: the masses, people, fame, food industry, mothers

Mercury: communications, trade, sales, computers, telephones, T.V., travel, advertising **Venus:** arts, music, luxuries, flowers, florist, make-up, perfume, vehicles **Mars:** weapons, real estate, cooking, sports, military, police **Jupiter:** teachers, lawyers, judges, ministers, travel long distance, astrologers **Saturn:** leaders, organizers, disciplinarians, sergeants

Rahu: computers, X-rays, poisons that heal, pharmaceuticals, alcohol, drugs, foreign items, foreign trade, aircraft

Ketu: spiritual, radiation, unusual careers, astrologers, unconventional, non-conformist, astrology

Neptune: film, movies, photographer, artist, poetry, mystical, psychic, oil, gas, alcohol, drugs, water, wine, oceans, ships, nautical navigator,

Uranus; astrology, aircraft, technology, inventions, computers, electricity, T.V., radios

Pluto: atomic energy, huge money, corporate take-overs, monopolies, power, control, sexual magnetism

2nd h. ♓	3rd h. ♈	4th h. ♉ ☊ 19:31 Roh ♅ 28:26 Mrg	5th h. ♊
1st h. ♒ Asc 24:22 PBh	Deepak Chopra Tue 10-22-1946 15:45:00 New Delhi, INDIA (general) India	Timezone: -5:30:00 DST: 0 Latitude: 28N36'00 Longitude: 77E12'00 Ayanamsha : -23:06:33 Lahiri	6th h. ♋ ♄ 14:59 Pus ♇ 20:07 Asl
12th h. ♑			7th h. ♌
11th h. ♐	10th h. ♏ ♀ 08:45 Anu ☋ 19:31 Jye	9th h. ♎ ☉ 05:17 Cht ♃ 12:37 Swa ♂ 25:59 Vis ☿ 27:22 Vis	8th h. ♍ ☽ 05:39 UPh ♆ 15:59 Has

Deepak Chopra started out as a medical doctor but ended up as a famous metaphysical teacher with many published books and speaking engagements worldwide. His ascendant is Aquarius which is ruled by Saturn. His Saturn resides in his 6th house of healing and service. He was initially drawn to the healing profession as he became a medical doctor. The 9th house stands out where 4 major planets reside. The 9th house rules philosophy, spirituality, teaching, and publishing. All the indicators of the 10 house of career are in the 9th house, Sun, Jupiter and Mars. The ruler of the 9th house is in the 10th house further indicating a 9th house career. When there is a connection of the 9th and the 10 houses this will bring luck and fortune to the individual concerning their career and social standing. He has the ruler of the 9th house, Venus in the 10th house in Scorpio which is ruled by Mars in the 9th house. They both exchanges signs with Mars in Libra the sign Venus rules and Venus in Scorpio the sign Mars rules. The connection of the 9th and 10th houses can produce fame. Deepak is a public speaker on spirituality and publishes many books.

He is a speaker and a writer of international acclaim. The 2nd house ruler Jupiter is how he makes his money. The 2nd house ruler in the 9th house means he makes his money in publishing and speaking on subjects of spirituality and philosophy. Mars as ruler of the 10th house of career also rules his 3rd house of writing. His acclaim is through his many published books on spirituality and healing.

The Moon in his 8th house and ruler of the 6th house of health and healing can represent his deep quest to uncover the truth in healing and can represent a doctor who does surgery.

Jupiter ruler of both the 2nd house and 11th house, is his great money producing planet. Jupiter is in the 9th house of luck, and opportunities. Jupiter in the 9th house aspects the 1st and the 5th houses, which empowers his creativity for writing plus, Mercury ruler of the 5th house is with Jupiter ruler of the money houses. This all adds up to wealth, money, and opportunities to speak and inspire others to explore his teachings of spiritual truth.

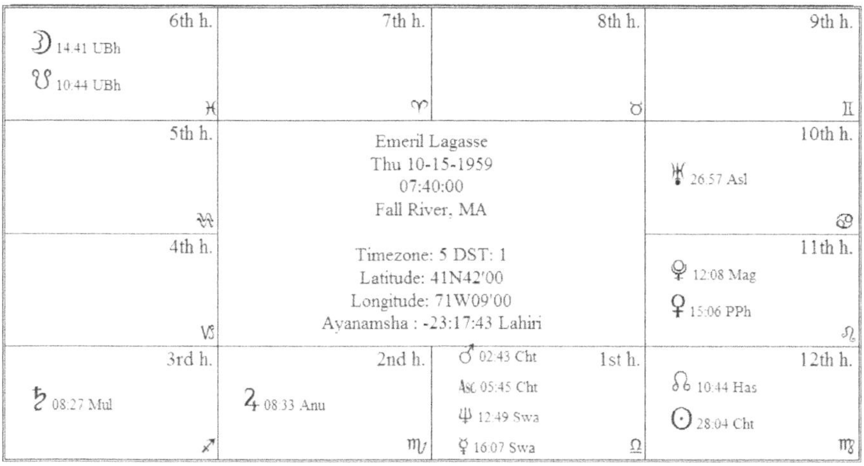

Emeril Lagasse is a very famous acclaimed chef. He is probably the most televised Chef in America. He has achieved the highest accolades in television as a chef. His show was recently bought by Martha Stewart for 50 million dollars. In Emeril's chart he has his Moon in the 6th house of the service industry. The Moon which rules his career house (10th) is in the 6th house of service. The 6th house can indicate healing as in doctors, nurses or nutrition and diet or food.

There are many indicators of wealth and fortune in this chart. Whenever the 2nd house connects to the 6th house many are drawn to the food industry. The 2nd house deals with how we make our money, but it also rules the mouth which indicates speech and eating. In this chart the ruler of the 6th house is in the 2nd house, and Emeril has made enormous money from his love of food and his showmanship with his cooking. He has Jupiter in the 2nd house of money and the ruler of the chart Venus (rules 1st house Libra) is in the 11 house of great gains.

He was born under a lunar eclipse with the Sun and Moon opposed with Rahu and Ketu. This will bring the person to the attention of the public through the houses this configuration takes place, and his is in the 6th house of service and the 12th house which rules institutions, such as restaurants. The 12th house usually indicates being behind the scenes, such as the kitchen and privacy.

It is surprising he became such a publicized figure on television, because he is really a very private person.

Mercury connects the 9th house with the 2nd house of money for they are conjunct in the 1st house this placement explains his notoriety. The 9th house is the house of blessings and the combination of the 9th house ruler with the 2nd house ruler will bring the wealth and blessings to him.

The ruler of the 11th house, the Sun is in the 12th house and aspects the Moon by opposition. Jupiter from the 2nd house is aspecting the Moon in the 6th house of work, service and cooking. This connects the 11th house with the 2nd house, the two houses of wealth and money, and when connected they will bring wealth to the individual through the profession that these houses indicate, food and cooking for Emeril.

9th h. ♓	10th h. ♈	11th h. ☊ 02:03 Kri ♉	12th h. ♅ 02:59 Mrg ♊
8th h. ♒	Stephen King Sun 09-21-1947 01:30:00 Portland, ME		1st h. ♂ 01:03 Pun Asc 06:44 Pus ♇ 21:07 Asl ♄ 24:59 Asl ♋
7th h. ♑	Timezone: 5 DST: 1 Latitude: 43N39'00 Longitude: 70W15'00 Ayanamsha : -23:07:22 Lahiri		2nd h. ♌
6th h. ♐	5th h. ♃ 00:40 Vis ☋ 02:03 Vis ☽ 23:07 Jye ♏	4th h. ♎	3rd h. ☉ 04:16 UPh ♀ 09:01 UPh ♆ 16:55 Has ☿ 21:54 Has ♍

Steven King is a prolific writer and screenwriter. As a former English teacher he achieved amazing notoriety. He wrote 40 successful horror novels by 1999, 26 movies were made from his books. He has grossed more than 100 million dollars per year. His books have sold over 100 million copies in 33 languages.

In terms of a career the 3rd house is the house of communications and a profession pertaining to writing. The 5th house is the house of talent and since the 5th house is the 3rd house from the 3rd house this indicates it is also a house for writing talents. Actually, the 5th house can mean writing books while the 3rd house is simply all writing ventures. Both houses together with powerful planets definitely point to a successful writer.

Focusing in on his 3rd house of communications and writing he has Mercury in its exalted sign Virgo. Mercury is placed next to mystical dreamy Neptune giving his writing deep imagination. Venus in the 3rd house is a bit weak in Virgo, but when a planet is debilitated with a planet that is exalted the weak planet is strengthened from the support of the exalted planet. Venus is ruler of the 11th house of great gains in the 3rd house of writing, plus the Sun ruler of the 2nd house is in the 3rd house with the 11th house ruler, Venus. Here is a great combination of both planets ruling the most important money houses 2 and 11 with exalted Mercury which just so happens to be the ruler of the 3rd house placed in the 3rd house. This is a dynamite combination of success, wealth and money through writing.

His 5th house is occupied by Jupiter with Ketu, giving him great depth with an enormously creative and intellectual mind. Jupiter rules his 9th house and resides in the 5th house of the mind and intelligence empowering his luck, fortune and talents. Additionally, his Mars and Moon are exchanged by being in each other's signs. This is a mutual reception, plus Jupiter aspects the Moon, Mars and Saturn. This connects the 1st, 5th and 9th houses to the houses of inspiration and luck. This is truly an amazing chart depicting this man's incredible writing skills, talents, mental qualities and the opportunities to get them out in the world for his ultimate success.

7th h. ♃ 21:57 Rev ♓	8th h. ☋ 27:24 Kri ♈	9th h. ♂℞ 24:02 Mrg ♉	10th h. ♊
6th h. ♒	Tiger Woods Tue 12-30-1975 22:50:00 Long Beach, Ca USA Timezone: 8 DST: 0 Latitude: 33N46'01 Longitude: 118W11'18 Ayanamsha : -23:31:32 Lahiri		11th h. ♄℞ 07:35 Pus ♋
5th h. ☿ 02:54 USh ♑			12th h. ♌
4th h. ☉ 15:26 PSh ♐	3rd h. ♀ 05:00 Anu ♆ 18:58 Jye ☽ 28:51 Jye ♏	2nd h. ♅ 12:49 Swa ☊ 27:24 Vis ♎	1st h. Asc 00:53 UPh ♇ 18:07 Has ♍

Tiger Woods has achieved the highest acclaim for golf in U.S. history to date. He is one of the most successful and highest paid athletes of our time. In the year 2000 he won all four championships, the Masters, the US Open, the British Open and the PGA. In 1997 he signed endorsements for Nike and Titleist for over 60 million dollars for over 5 years. Currently, his fortune has grown to over the billionaire mark.

Sports that take a certain amount of finesse and talent will exemplify the 3rd and 5th houses. These houses have been seen before for great communication skills and talent. And if the athlete is successful in terms of financial rewards the 2nd and the 11th houses must come into play. Again with someone with incredible skills and talents we see an extraordinary 3rd house. Here is the ruler of both money houses 2 and 11 in the 3rd house. This explicitly means the person becomes wealthy through their talents and skills using their hands. The 3rd house rules the hands as in writing and in their use in any creative endeavor. Golf uses the manipulation of the hands like most sports. Neptune can sometimes mean some kind of special gift from beyond this world. His Mars also aspects this house and it rules the sign Scorpio so it is aspecting a house it rules, meaning it strengthens this house all the more for the attributes this house rules. Additionally, Jupiter aspects this house and the planet's there in, Venus, Moon and Neptune. This house is full of gifts, talents and is fortified to the ultimate, from Mars and Jupiter.

The sign Scorpio can be very passionate and the Nakshatra Jyestha is here as well. This is the nakshatra I have found most often in the charts of billionaires. The other one is Vishaka and he has Rahu here in the 2nd house. Rahu magnifies the placements it resides in, and this is the house of money.

He has Mercury in the 5th house of talent and intelligence. This is the house of the mind and he has to have a very calculating mind to be this successful in such an individualistic sport. Mercury rules his Virgo ascendant. This connects the 1st house with the 5th house. This gives inspiration and luck. Saturn aspects the 5th house by opposition and it is aspecting Mercury which gives the mind a very deep contemplative focus that one would need to excel in this sport. Saturn is aspecting the sign on the 5th house Capricorn, and it rules Capricorn so it powers up this house all the more with its concentration of mental focus and power.

Notice when individuals have a chart where the 3rd, 7th and 11th houses are aspected by Jupiter, (Jupiter is in one of these houses), the person is successful from all 3 of these houses. The trine of Jupiter connects these houses indicating the individual will be talented and will have opportunities through the empowered 11th house to express the talent and receive rewards. In Tiger's chart Jupiter in his 7th house aspects the 3rd house planets plus Saturn in the 11th house of gains. His destiny was certain with this powerful chart for skills, talent and mental focus.

12th h. ♓	1st h. ☿ 04:40 Ash Asc 14:27 Bha ☉ 15:19 Bha ♈	2nd h. ♀ 07:23 Kri ♉	3rd h. ♃ 01:44 Mrg ☋ 24:13 Pun ♅ 26:14 Pun ♊
11th h. ☽ 26:51 PBh ♒	Jerry Seinfeld Thu 04-29-1954 06:00:00 Brooklyn, NY		4th h. ♇ 29:19 Asl ♋
10th h. ♑	Timezone: 5 DST: 1 Latitude: 40N38'00 Longitude: 73W56'00 Ayanamsha : -23:13:24 Lahiri		5th h. ♌
9th h. ☊ 24:13 PSh ♂ 12:03 Mul ♐	8th h. ♏	7th h. ♆ 01:05 Cht ♄℞ 12:37 Swa ♎	6th h. ♍

Jerry Seinfeld is one of the highest paid TV comedians of our time. In terms of what constitutes what is funny in a chart I usually refer to the sign Gemini. To be funny you have to sharp and quick witted. You have to be smart to be funny, because your mind has to think quickly and be a head of everyone in a conversation. Mercury is the planet that rules the trickster in Greek mythology and also rules the mental disposition. In Gemini the mind is quick and adaptable. The sign Virgo which is also ruled by Mercury produces a more dry humor. Great comedians will have a powerful Mercury. Seinfeld has Jupiter in the sign Gemini in the 3rd house. Jupiter is accentuated by Ketu in the 3rd house. The 3rd house is about communications and the arts, and Jerry has a powerful skill to come across dramatically with his stage act.

In terms of wealth and money Jerry has Venus, the planet of opulent wealth, in its own sign of rulership in the 2nd house of money. The 2nd house also rules our voice and Jerry uses his voice most eloquently to deliver his comedic punches.

For people in the entertainment business the 5th house should be assessed for it rules entertainment, drama, talent, and showman ship. The ruler of his 5th house is exalted meaning his abilities are supreme. The Sun resides in his 1st house indicating his abilities are presented in his physical demeanor.

The 11th house is ruled by Saturn and Saturn is in the 7th house (angular) exalted. Both the 2nd and the 11th house are ruled by planets in their strongest signs to produce high results. Furthermore, Jupiter aspects the 11th house and the Moon there in the 11th house. Jupiter also aspects exalted Saturn in the 7th house. Jupiter expands and multiplies the houses and planets it aspects. Venus is connected to Saturn because Saturn is in the sign Libra which rules Venus.

The 9th house of luck and fortune is aspected by Jupiter and Jupiter rules the sign Sagittarius on the 9th house. When a planet aspects a house that it rules, it magnifies the power of the house to produce what that house is good for, and it is good for luck and good fortune.

Chapter 8

How to use Astrology for the Stock Market

"It's common knowledge that a large percentage of Wall Street brokers use astrology. "
Donald Reagan, formerly Ronald Reagan's Chief of Staff

Over the years I have studied with some of the most brilliant astrologers who have made this into a science. They have newsletters, software programs and books to help those who want to make money. But with so many variables there is not a flawless formula. It is mind boggling all the details that have to be considered. You have to be proficient in both astrology and stock market trading.

Here is how it all starts and how I use astrology for the stock market. First a company or business opens for business, then it incorporates, and begins to sell shares to the public, then an underwriter will line up the buyers, this is the initial offering (IPO). This means the stock has gone public. About 5 days after the stock opens trading it is listed on the New York Stock Exchange (NYSE). The IPO and first trade date are close together but the first trade date is the birth of the stock on the stock market and is the time to use.

The way that traders use astrology is to take the day and time that the particular stock you are interested in was first traded on the stock market. This is the first trade date. This in essence is the birth of that company's stock first entering the stock market.

Astrology is simply a map of the planets for the day, year, time and place of birth. This can be applied to the birth or beginning of anything. Everything has a beginning and an end. Therefore, a chart can be calculated for the birth of a person, the birth or beginning of any event such as the beginning or start of a business, marriage, moving into a house, the start of a trip, the start of a job, or time of a surgery, anything you would want to know the outcome for.

The time a stock is first traded on in the stock market is definitely accurate, for the time of the first trade is documented and this information is easily found. The place is always New York City at 9:30 AM when the stock market opens now for trade. The New York stock exchange (NYSE) began trading at 10 AM until September 30th 1985, but changed after this date to 9:30

AM. Of course this refers to the American stock market, other countries will have this information available as well.

Once the chart has been erected for the day, year, time and place, of this first trade date then what is observed are certain planets in this chart. Each planet represents certain things. Then houses will reveal specific information according to what they rule. But the real trick is to look at where the planets are currently in the heavens to understand what will actually happen to this stock. The movements of the planets as they move in the sky are called Transits. It is very simple to observe the planets as the move in the sky and compare the relationship to the planets at the time of the birth of the stock's first trade chart.

The 12 Planets Used in 1st Trade Charts

Sun: The boss, President, or the CEO of the company, it is a focal point in the chart, and represents the energy and soul of the company

Moon: The public, popularity, instability and changes

Mercury: Communications in a business, trade and travel business, press release and publicity

Venus: Good reputation, beauty products, luxury items such as cars, boats, and interior decor

Mars: Energy, makes stocks move, real estate, technical equipment, engineers, weapons,

Jupiter: Expansion, excesses, expansion, upward trends, education, travel

Saturn: Restriction, setbacks, downward trends, stability and reliable

Uranus: Change, sudden ups and downs, volatility, sudden trends with extremes, airplanes, computers, electricity

Neptune: Deceptive price moves, dissolves things, confusion, water, liquids, oil, gas, oceans, drugs, alcohol

Pluto: Substantial price moves, takeovers, extremes, power struggles, control, manipulation

Rahu: Fame, power, worldly success, obsessions, extremes, foreigners

Ketu: Loss, spiritual, death, illusions, fantasy

Aspects

Aspects are the MOST important part of astrology to understand if you want to make real money. The aspects are the degrees between the planets that make them powerful or weak, and actually create the events concerning the rise or fall in the stock market.

There are 360 degrees in the zodiac and the aspects are measurements of these degrees' distance between the planets.

We will be looking at the degrees between the planets in charts and then we will add the planets transiting in the sky to this birth chart (first trade chart), The aspects between the planets in the birth chart to the current position in the sky will determine the trends in the stock. In actuality these aspects are not good or bad they simply indicate when a stock will rise or fall, and with this knowledge you will make money. Buy when it falls and sell when it rises.

Most Powerful Aspects

Conjunction: 0 degrees; Intensity, activation, big events, depending on the planets involved it may be for good or bad, This brings the 2 energies together and creates an event

Square: 90 degrees; hard, difficult, obstacles and setbacks, brings lows

Trine: 120 degrees: Brings ease and comfort, and luck, will move a stock upward

Quincunx: 150 degrees; Complications, Problems for a stock, may indicate a long low trend

Opposition: 180 degrees: Up and down trend very volatile,

Here is another way to find these aspects with more detail. Take the degree of the planet and count the number of signs it is to the next planet in question. This includes more obscure aspects. The aspects listed above are the strongest aspects to note.

1 (Conjunction), In the same

2 sign signs away: (Semi Sextile) Conflict and can cause a small rise with a greater fall

3 signs away: (Sextile) Positive and can be a quick but temporary rise

4 signs away: (Square) Major block so the stock will shift downward

5 signs away: (Trine) Sudden rise from a standstill

6 signs away: (Quincunx) Difficulty and standstill, obstacles for the stock

7 signs away: (Opposition): Conflict, stock teetering back and forth, not much movement

8 signs away: (Quincunx): Difficulty and standstill, obstacles for the stock

9 signs away: (Trine): Sudden rise from a standstill

10 signs away: (Square) Major block so the stock will shift downward

11 signs away: (Sextile) Positive and can be a quick but temporary rise

12 signs away: (Semi Sextile) Small conflict and can cause a small rise with a greater fall

Houses: In First Trade Charts

Here you will understand how the numbers of the houses closely relate to the numbers of the aspects. Planets in each house determine if it will prosper or be problematic.

1st house: the beginning, the essence of the business

2nd House; Money, financial situation of the business/stock

3rd House: Communications, information, education

4th House: Property, home, real estate, foundation of the company

5th House: Good results, happiness, speculation, games, gambling, sports

6th House: Enemies, obstacles, debts, struggle

7th House: The opponent, business mergers, partners

8th House: Death, investors, others money, scandals

9th House: Flow and movement, luck, law, legal, lawyers

10th House: success, open to the public, leaders, government

11th House: gains through business

12th House: endings, loss, closure

The Houses that give the best results for a business are 1,5, and 9

The houses that are related the gains in money are 2, 5, 9, and 11

The houses that cause the most problems are 6, 8 and 12

The 8th house can indicate money from other sources outside the company (sometimes a takeover)

Signs

The signs that the planets are in are very important in terms of what signs planets prosper in or are depleted or weak in. Planets in a weak sign will not give the results expected for good or a rise, and planets in a weak sign will cause lows or long standing low trends. Listed here are the signs in their order of strength and weakness.

*When a planet is in the strongest sign it will be extreme, especially concerning expansion

*When a planet is in the weakest sign it will be extremely depressed

*Pay special attention to the strongest and weakest signs.

Sun

Strongest Signs: Aries, Leo
Strong: Cancer, Scorpio, Sagittarius, Pisces
Weakest: Libra
Weak: Taurus, Gemini, Virgo, Capricorn, Aquarius

Moon

Strongest: Taurus, Cancer
Strong: Aries, Leo, Sagittarius, Pisces
Weakest: Scorpio
Weak: Gemini, Virgo, Libra, Capricorn, Aquarius

Mercury

Strongest: Virgo, Gemini
Strong; Taurus, Libra, Capricorn, Aquarius
Weakest: Pisces
Weak: Aries, Cancer, Leo, Scorpio, Sagittarius

Venus

Strongest: Pisces, Taurus, Libra
Strong: Gemini, Capricorn, Aquarius
Weakest: Virgo
Weak: Aries, Cancer, Leo, Scorpio, Sagittarius

Mars

Strongest: Capricorn, Aries, Scorpio
Strong: Cancer, Leo, Sagittarius, Pisces

Weakest: Cancer
Weak: Taurus, Gemini, Virgo, Libra, Aquarius

Jupiter

Strongest: Cancer, Sagittarius, Pisces Strong: Aries, Leo, Scorpio,
Weakest: Capricorn
Weak: Taurus, Gemini, Virgo, Libra, Aquarius

Saturn

Strongest: Libra, Capricorn, Aquarius
Strong: Taurus, Gemini, Virgo,

Weakest: Aries
Weak: Cancer, Leo, Scorpio, Sagittarius, Pisces

Uranus

Strongest: Aquarius
Weakest: Leo

Neptune

Strongest: Pisces
Weakest: Virgo

Pluto

Strongest: Scorpio
Weakest: Taurus

Eclipses

Erratic shifts in the stock market occur during the times of the Eclipses. Eclipses occur twice a year, six months apart. The solar eclipse is the focus while a lunar eclipse is part of the cycle. The lunar eclipse will occur 2 weeks before or after, and sometimes both before and after a Solar Eclipse. The lunar eclipse is a Full Moon and the solar eclipse is a New Moon. The difference between and eclipse and a new or full Moon is that they line up with the Lunar Nodes. For an eclipse to occur the Sun and Moon must be within an 18 degree orb of the lunar nodes (Rahu and Ketu). The nodes in Vedic astrology are called Rahu (North Node) and Ketu (South Node). So, an eclipse is a New Moon that lines up and occurs twice a year six months apart. Actually it is the degree of the Lunar Nodes that will mark the volatility in the stock market. This is an **extremely** important key to mark the extremes of the stock market. Where these eclipses occur will indicate the most volatile area of the stock or business, and when they conjoin planets in these charts *Big* changes are about to occur.

Slow Moving Planets

The slower a planet moves the more intense the energy, and the longer some of the effects will last. The 3 outer planets Uranus, Neptune, and Pluto move the slowest and will give long range effects, but Saturn and Jupiter are the true markers of where the market will go. Mars can be the factor that energizes the planets it aspects, and creates ups and downs. The small triggers are the faster moving planets, Sun, Venus, Mercury and the Moon.

Planetary Stations

Another very specific feature to pay attention to is when a planet stations and turns retrograde or direct. At this time a planet appears to standstill in the sky. This is extremely important and will create major changes. Because when a planet changes directions so does the stock market. The planets that shift directions will pertain to the areas the planet rules.

Important Rules

1. Eclipses will cause major shifts in the stock market.
2. Slower moving planets make a bigger impact.
3. Stations of planets create changes in the stock market.
4. Jupiter and Saturn determine the social climate of the stock market from year to year.

5. Aspects of Mars energizes the planets it aspects.
6. Faster moving planets are small triggers.
7. The aspects or degrees between the planets transiting to the natal planets are what cause the changes in the stock market.

The Secret to Astrological Cycles

What you are about to discover will explain the secrets of the cycles of Earth and humanity. On this planet Earth there are cycles and patterns that can be understood and analyzed to make sense of the future cycles. Astrology is the tool to understand these patterns, and they can be applied across all patterns or cycles of our lives. The charts of the business' first trade chart are here to give credence to the theory that the Nodal Axis of Rahu and Ketu are very specific to the extremes of the highest price of the stock to the lowest. Rahu and Ketu take around 18 and a half years to make a complete revolution through the entire zodiac, but the half cycle of 9 years was the reversal from high to low or low to high.

<table>
<tr><td>9th h.
♓</td><td>10th h.
♈</td><td>11th h.
♃ 00:36 Kri
♀℞ 23:04 Roh
☿℞ 24:40 Mrg
♉</td><td>12th h.
☉ 07:38 Ard
♊</td></tr>
<tr><td>8th h.
♂ 25:16 PBh
☊ 23:34 PBh
♒</td><td colspan="2" rowspan="2">Dell Computers
Wed 06-22-1988
09:30:00
New York, NY
USA
Timezone: 5 DST: 1
Latitude: 40N42'51
Longitude: 74W00'23
Ayanamsha : -23:41:49 Lahiri</td><td>1st h.
Asc 26:27 Asl
♋</td></tr>
<tr><td>7th h.
♑</td><td>2nd h.
☋ 23:34 PPh
♌</td></tr>
<tr><td>6th h.
♆ 15:19 PSh
♄℞ 05:23 Mul
♅ 05:15 Mul
♐</td><td>5th h.
♏</td><td>4th h.
♇ 16:16 Swa
♎</td><td>3rd h.
☽ 09:03 UPh
♍</td></tr>
</table>

April 2000 Dell stock sold for $50.13 a share. At this time transiting Rahu was 5 degrees of Cancer and transiting Ketu was 5 degrees of Capricorn. Transiting Jupiter and Saturn were conjunct in Aries in the 10th house. This was a record high for this stock!

January 2009 Dell stock sold at $9.50 a share. At this time transiting Rahu was 15 degrees of Capricorn and Transiting Ketu was 15 degrees of Cancer. Jupiter was transiting with Rahu and transiting Saturn was in Leo in the 2nd house of money with natal Ketu. This is a very bad combination. But the most relevant point here is that the transiting nodes are in the opposite place as when there was the high point for this stock 9 years later. This was a record low.

3rd h. ♓	4th h. ♈	5th h. ♉	6th h. ♊
2nd h. ♒	Apple Computers Fri 12-12-1980 10:00:00 New York, NY USA Timezone: 5 DST: 0 Latitude: 40N42'51 Longitude: 74W00'23 Ayanamsha : -23:35:14 Lahiri		7th h. ☊ 18:25 Asl ♋
1st h. ☽ 26:20 Dha ☋ 18:25 Shr Asc 08:42 USh ♑			8th h. ♌
12th h. ♂ 22:08 PSh ♐	11th h. ♅ 03:46 Anu ☿ 16:49 Jye ☉ 27:10 Jye ♆ 28:44 Jye ♏	10th h. ♇ 00:09 Cht ♀ 29:23 Vis ♎	9th h. ♃ 14:00 Has ♄ 14:59 Has ♍

Apple Computers stock sold at $7.44 December 2000. At this time transiting Rahu was 22 degrees of Gemini and Ketu was 22 degrees Sagittarius. Transiting Jupiter and Saturn were conjunct in Taurus. This was one of the lowest trends for this stock.

Apple Computer stock sold for $259.00 a share July 2010. During this time transiting Rahu was 17 degrees Sagittarius and transiting Ketu was 17 degrees of Gemini. Again in a 9 year cycle where the nodal axis reverses the stock will shift from low to high. Transiting Saturn and Jupiter are opposed with Saturn in Virgo and Jupiter in Pisces. This is the highest price for this stock to date.

12th h. ♀ 11:56 UBh ☿℞ 05:01 UBh ♓	1st h. ☽ 04:01 Ash ☊ 06:41 Ash Asc 27:33 Kri ♈	2nd h. ♉	3rd h. ♊
11th h. ☉ 29:05 PBh ♃ 11:20 Sat ♒	Microsoft Thu 03-13-1986 09:30:00 Dallas, TX USA Timezone: 6 DST: 0 Latitude: 32N47'00 Longitude: 96W48'00 Ayanamsha : -23:39:43 Lahiri		4th h. ♋
10th h. ♑			5th h. ♌
9th h. ♆ 11:58 Mul ♐	8th h. ♄ 16:00 Anu ♅ 28:37 Jye ♂ 28:44 Jye ♏	7th h. ☋ 06:41 Swa ♇ 13:23 Swa ♎	6th h. ♍

Microsoft's stock sold for $58.00 December 1999. During this time transiting Rahu was 10 degrees of Cancer and transiting Ketu was 10 degrees of Capricorn. Transiting Jupiter and Saturn were conjunct in Aries. This was a high point for this stock.

March of 2009 Microsoft's stock is an extreme low selling for $18. During this time again the nodes of the Moon Rahu and Ketu reversed. Transiting Rahu was in Capricorn and transiting Ketu was in Cancer. Transiting Jupiter was with Rahu in Capricorn and transiting Saturn was 23 degrees Leo.

More than any planetary aspect the nodes of the Moon have proved their value in predicting long range stock cycles. They can be charted as they relate to the cycles of Jupiter and Saturn to get reliable results as to the trends of stocks in the stock market. To see the shorter range then the half cycles are broken down. The half cycle of the half cycle of Rahu and Ketu is four and a half years. This will trigger changes within the long haul of the 9 year half cycle. Also, the conjunctions and oppositions of both Jupiter and Saturn must be watched. Jupiter and Saturn conjunct every 20 years and they will oppose half way between the conjunctions which is 10 years after the conjunction. Furthermore, the cycle of Jupiter with Rahu/Ketu are important for Jupiter will conjunct Ketu then Rahu every 3 and a half or 4 years. Therefore, Jupiter will conjoin Rahu every 8 years but it will conjunct Ketu half way between the 8 years which is 3-4 years.

Saturn will conjunct Rahu every 12-13 years and will conjoin Ketu half way between which is every 6 years following the conjunction to Rahu.

These are the specific cycles to be watched to find the highs and lows and the trends a stock will make with the cycle of the 9 years of the half cycle of the full 18 and a half cycle of Rahu ad Ketu. These cycles are plotted across the history of The United States of America from 1920- 2050, *Chapter 5: Past Astrological Timelines Reveal the Future*

Chapter 9
How to Predict a Sudden Rise in Life

"Lottery Winners"
"The natures and dispositions of men are, not without truth, distinguished from the predominance of the planets."

Sir Francis Bacon

Initially, when one begins the study of astrology it is believed that all events can be predicted in a chart. The chart is a map of the karmas of a soul. There is a promise indicated in every chart but the probability of it all coming to fruition is definitely tempered by the fact that we all have free will. But some events seem predestined. It is our choices and how we operate within the apparent destined events of life that can shift our soul development. Much of our free will is developed through our thinking process for we can choose how we think and the choices we make *within* the apparent destined events. I believe some events are fated or predestined and our choices within these events can shape and change our lives.

The curse of Shiva claims that Lord Shiva felt that astrologers were somehow interfering with free will, and put a curse on them. Essentially he declared that astrologers would never agree with each other. In my opinion this is a symbolic story to help us understand we have free will and the planets reveal indications and cannot be totally predicable.

The great gum preceptor Paramahansa Yogananda said there is nothing stronger then the will of man. He respects the science of astrology but maintains that we have a certain amount of free will that can overcome the forces of the planets.

The trance medium Edgar Cayce also believes that astrology is well and true but there is nothing more powerful that the will of man and he repeatedly claims we can change our lives through our will and thoughts.

And most people would agree that if everything were predestined then there would be absolutely no purpose or meaning for life if we were all puppets acting out a script with no variation or choice.

Our choices that we make within the parameters of these predestined events determine our spiritual growth and can invariably change the course of our life. Will we achieve happiness or misfortune through our opportunities of sudden luck and fortune? Likewise, our choices in times of a great fall from grace and difficulty are also events that will give us the opportunity for choices to be made and will determine our future circumstances and karma. We have free will and the choices made when a fortune suddenly occurs will determine our future karma, resulting in happiness or misfortune. I believe it is important to know that any life changing event is an opportunity for spiritual growth. There is no other reason for our experiences here, but to come to a realization of higher consciousness and connection to our Divinity. All life events lead us to this realization.

Variables Considered in Understanding the Prediction of a Sudden Rise in Fortune: Why the Trine Aspect is Important for Luck.

1) Aspect that promotes luck and fortune is the trine, which is 120 degrees or 5 or 9 placements (signs/houses) from planets.

2) In Vedic astrology Jupiter is the planet of luck and fortune and its full aspect is the trine.

3) Houses that promote luck and fortune are the trikonal houses which are 1, 5, and 9, they are called the trikonal houses. This reinforces the theory of the lucky aspect of the trine (120 degrees).

4) Each nakshatra is ruled by a planet. There are 9 planets, and each of them rule 3 nakshatras. The nakshatras that are ruled by the same planet are 120 degrees from each other or trine each other in the zodiac. For example the nakshatras Ashwini, Magha and Mula are ruled by Ketu. All 3 are in the beginning of Fire signs, which trine each other. When one nakshatra is activated with a transiting planet it activates the other nakshatras ruled by the same planet. Simply meaning they are in trine to each other (120 degrees).

5) It is believed by most Vedic astrologers that the full aspect of both Rahu and Ketu is the 5, 9 aspect which is the trine aspect of 120 degrees. Rahu and Ketu definitely predict major changes within life. There are many variables involved in predicting the effects of these.

6) Therefore; Jupiter and Rahu and Ketu cast the same full aspect, 5, 9 or 120 degrees (Trine).

7) All these points emphasize the importance of the trine aspect. Particularly in predicting favorable events.

8) When there are three points that are 120 degrees from each other, they form a grand trine in the chart. The points will be in the same element and in the 3 nakshatras that are ruled by the same planet, close in degree.

Similarities in the aspect of Rahu/Ketu and Jupiter:

a) Jupiter and Rahu/Ketu cast trines for a full aspect

b) Jupiter has 2 stations a year, (stationary retrograde and stationary direct) Rahu/Ketu have 2 eclipses a year, where they station.

c) Jupiter travels retrograde approximately 9-10 degrees backwards in the zodiac while Rahu/Ketu travel approximately 9-12 degrees backwards at each eclipse per year (12 months apart).

- When Jupiter and Rahu aspect one another they cast a trine and aspect the other point simultaneously creating a grand trine in a chart. Natal planets aspected by the transiting grand trine create sudden wind falls of luck.

Rahu and Ketu appear to station and remain the same degree for 2-3 months twice a year at the time of the solar eclipse. This is using the True Nodes, which tracks the real movements of the lunar nodes. I do not use the mean nodes which are estimated points of the lunar nodes. It is believed that planets that cross this degree after the eclipse mark the occurrence of events. Some believe it is the degree of the eclipse that marks the sensitive point, which is the degree of the New moon at the time of an eclipse. I believe it is the station of the lunar nodes that is more significant.

The signs also activated are the signs in trine from both transiting Jupiter and the transiting lunar nodes (Rahu/Ketu). The degree that Jupiter makes its station prior to the event is very sensitive to transits passing over that degree, as well as the stationing degree of Rahu/Ketu. These degrees seem to be activated in events of great magnitude. Both the stationary retrograde and stationary direct degree of Jupiter are significant. Because, when a planet stands still it is at its most powerful position.

Charts of large lottery wins will prove the theory of the aspects of transiting Jupiter and Rahu/Ketu and there stationary points.

Explanation of Stations

When a planet stands still it is at its point of power. When a planet changes direction in the retrograde process it appears to stand still, this is called a station. These are points of power and must be noted. The points of Jupiter and Rahu as they station prior to an event become very sensitive zones. These degrees of a station mark a very sensitive spot and react like a land mine. When a planet crosses over or aspects these sensitive points an event occurs. These degrees stay active till another retrograde cycle occurs, then a new sensitive point is created. In these examples the sensitive station points will be observed. The stationary points for Jupiter are when Jupiter turns retrograde and when Jupiter turns direct. There is only one time a year that Jupiter turns retrograde and another where Jupiter turns direct. So there are 2 stationary points to consider. Jupiter is retrograde about 4 months of the year and travels approximately 10 degrees backwards in the zodiac when retrograde. Therefore, the stationary direct degree will occur about 4 months after the retrograde point and will be 10 degrees earlier than the degree Jupiter turned retrograde.

Rahu and Ketu appear to station when there is an eclipse. The lunar nodes seem to stand still or station for about 2-3 months. This occurs twice a year when we have the solar eclipse 6 months apart. This is when Rahu and Ketu are most powerful and create a sensitive point in the zodiac, and when a transit crosses over it an event occurs. When a natal planet is aspected tightly in orb by these transiting station degrees an event occurs in the individual's life.

All these variables are considered in terms of the events that occur at the times of life changing events.

As an astrologer I am well aware there are many factors to consider for a prediction but for the simplicity of proving this theory we are taking into account only these variables.

Points Analyzed in Charts

1) Transiting Jupiter to natal planets (Conjunctions and forming trines) in close proximity.
2) Transiting lunar nodes, Rahu and Ketu to natal planets (conjunctions and forming trines) in close proximity.
3) Transiting Jupiter to transiting Rahu and Ketu. (conjunctions and trines)

4) Prior stations either stationary retrograde and stationary direct degrees of Jupiter that occur before the event. When close to natal planets and activated by aspecting transiting planets an event occurs. If they station close to a natal planet then the effects will occur concerning this natal planet, house it is in and house it rules.

5) Prior stations of Rahu/Ketu that occur around the time of the eclipse. These degrees are powerful points in the chart to be activated by aspecting transits and when close to natal planets can create an event.

6) Another point that consistently appeared in the events was the connection of the transiting lunar nodes, Rahu and Ketu aspecting their natal positions.

7) Natal or transiting Saturn is involved many times with the transits of Rahu/Ketu or Jupiter.

<table>
<tr><td>8th h.
♓</td><td>9th h.
♃ 22:58 Bha
♈</td><td>10th h.
☊ 28:53 Mrg
♉</td><td>11th h.
♊</td></tr>
<tr><td>7th h.
♄ 10:03 Sat
♒</td><td colspan="2" rowspan="2">Debra Houle
Thu 01-21-1965
19:13:00
Philadelphia, PA
USA
Timezone: 5 DST: 0
Latitude: 39N57'08
Longitude: 75W09'51
Ayanamsha : -23:21:53 Lahiri</td><td>12th h.
♋</td></tr>
<tr><td>6th h.
☉ 08:24 USh
♑</td><td>1st h.
Asc 04:12 Mag
♅ 20:59 PPh
♇ 22:39 PPh
♌</td></tr>
<tr><td>5th h.
♀ 18:43 PSh
☿ 18:17 PSh
♐</td><td>4th h.
☋ 28:53 Jye
♏</td><td>3rd h.
♆ 26:24 Vis
♎</td><td>2nd h.
♂ 04:23 UPh
☽ 08:46 UPh
♍</td></tr>
</table>

Debra Houle won 26 million dollars 04/04/1997. On that day transiting Jupiter was 21 degrees Capricorn, transiting Rahu was 4 degrees Virgo. Rahu was conjunct natal Mars in the 2nd house of money and Mars rules the 9th house of luck and fortune. Plus transiting Jupiter in Capricorn was aspecting transiting Rahu and natal Rahu. There is a grand trine involving transiting Rahu, Jupiter, aspecting natal Mars, Moon, Sun and Rahu.

Transiting Jupiter turned Stationary retrograde in June 1997 at 28 degrees Capricorn. Rahu stationed at 4 degrees Capricorn. Transiting Jupiter stationed at 28 Capricorn, casting the trine aspect to natal Rahu at 28 degrees Taurus. Generally the station of Jupiter is taken into account before the event, but in this case this indicates the results of the lottery win, after the money was received.

Transiting Rahu stationed at 4 degrees Virgo conjoining natal Mars. Additionally, the grand trine is occurring in Artha houses, earth signs denoting money.

10th h. ☉ 29:25 Rev ♀ 09:26 UBh ♓	11th h. ☿ 18:50 Bha ♈	12th h. ♅ 13:14 Roh ♄ 28:59 Mrg ♉	1st h. Asc 00:25 Mrg ♂ 14:43 Ard ♊
9th h. ♒	Russell D. Clark Wed 04-12-1944 09:21:00 Weymouth, MA USA Timezone: 5 DST: 1 Latitude: 42N13'15 Longitude: 70W56'25 Ayanamsha : -23:04:28 Lahiri		2nd h. ☊ 09:52 Pus ♇ 13:20 Pus ♃℞ 23:57 Asl ♋
8th h. ☋ 09:52 USh ♑			3rd h. ♌
7th h. ♐	6th h. ☽ 14:06 Anu ♏	5th h. ♎	4th h. ♆ 09:16 UPh ♍

Russell Clark won 3 million dollars on 11/16/1991.

On that day transiting Jupiter was 17 degrees Leo and Rahu was 17 degrees Sagittarius. They are both trine each other and natal Mercury at 18 degrees of Aries completing a grand trine. Mercury is in the 11th house of great gains.

But the last retrograde period for Jupiter was March 1991 at that time transiting Jupiter turned Stationary direct at 9 degrees of Cancer which was conjunct natal Rahu in the 2nd house of money. Interestingly enough transiting Saturn activated this point too because on the day of the win transiting Saturn was 8 degrees of Capricorn on natal Ketu aspecting Rahu in the 2nd house the degree stationary Jupiter last marked.

5th h. ♓	6th h. ☽ 18:25 Bha ♈	7th h. ☊ 03:06 Kri ♉	8th h. ♅ 02:44 Mrg ♂ 21:32 Pun ♊
4th h. ♒	Rosemarie Bowser Fri 09-05-1947 13:16:00 Boston, MA USA Timezone: 5 DST: 1 Latitude: 42N21'30 Longitude: 71W03'37 Ayanamsha : -23:07:21 Lahiri		9th h. ♇ 20:44 Asl ♄ 23:12 Asl ♋
3rd h. ♑			10th h. ☉ 19:09 PPh ♀ 19:44 PPh ☿ 26:07 PPh ♌
2nd h. ♐	1st h. ☋ 03:06 Vis Asc 10:27 Anu ♏	12th h. ♃ 28:20 Vis ♎	11th h. ♆ 16:22 Has ♍

Rosemary Bowser won 13 million on 12/22/1984

On that day transiting Jupiter was 25 degrees Sagittarius forming a grand trine with the natal Moon 18 degrees Aries and Sun/Venus, 19 degrees Leo and Mercury at 26 degrees Leo. Transiting Jupiter was in the 2nd house of money.

The prior stationary retrograde of Jupiter was 19 degrees Sagittarius in April 1984. It is exactly in trine to the Sun and Venus.

Transiting Rahu was 3 degrees of Taurus, conjunct the natal Rahu at 3 degrees of Taurus. Additionally, transiting Saturn is at 0 degrees of Scorpio conjunct natal Ketu, aspecting both transiting and natal Rahu.

8th h. ♓	9th h. ♈	10th h. ♉	11th h. ♊
♀ 28:28 Rev ♂ 21:02 Rev ☿ 02:24 PBh	♃ 22:08 Bha		♅ 21:28 Pun
7th h. ♒ ☉ 14:52 Sat	Richard Harrington Thu 02-26-1953 18:22:00 Boston, MA USA Timezone: 5 DST: 0 Latitude: 42N21'30 Longitude: 71W03'37 Ayanamsha : -23:12:24 Lahiri		12th h. ♋ ☋ 19:07 Asl ☽ 25:14 Asl ♇ 28:27 Asl
6th h. ♑ ☊ 19:07 Shr			1st h. ♌ Asc 25:49 PPh
5th h. ♐	4th h. ♏	3rd h. ♎ ♆ 00:23 Cht ♄R 03:40 Cht	2nd h. ♍

Richard Harrington won 4 million on 12/23/2002

On that day transiting Jupiter was 23 degrees Cancer and Rahu was 14 degrees of Taurus, and transiting Ketu at 14 degrees of Scorpio trines transiting Jupiter. Transiting Jupiter is conjunct natal Moon/Ketu forming a trine to the 8th house planets in Pisces, Venus, Mars and Mercury. The 8th house is frequently involved in lottery wins since it rules unearned money, such as inheritances and insurance.

Transiting Ketu completes the grand trine with 14 degrees of Scorpio. Transiting Rahu is trine natal Rahu as well in earth signs in Artha houses representing money matters.

The stations of both Jupiter and Rahu were about the same degrees that they were at the time of the lottery win. Jupiter was stationary retrograde in December at 24 degrees of Cancer and Rahu was 14 degrees of Taurus. This empowered these degrees. The natal Moon is directly on this station of Jupiter.

6th h. ♓	7th h. ♃ 24:38 Bha ♈	8th h. ♉	9th h. ♅ 22:13 Pun ♊
5th h. ♒	Shirley May Sat 07-26-1952 14:10:00 Cambridge, MA USA		10th h. ☉ 10:28 Pus ♀ 19:15 Asl ♇ 27:25 Asl ☋ 28:22 Asl ♋
4th h. ☊ 28:22 Dha ♑	Timezone: 5 DST: 1 Latitude: 42N22'00 Longitude: 71W06'00 Ayanamsha : -23:11:52 Lahiri		11th h. ☿ 03:34 Mag ♌
3rd h. ♐	2nd h. ♏	1st h. ♂ 19:49 Swa Asc 20:03 Vis ♎	12th h. ☽ 02:25 UPh ♄ 16:42 Has ♆ 25:55 Cht ♍

Shirley May won 3 million on 12/26/1991

On that day transiting Jupiter was 20 degrees Leo and transiting Rahu was 16 degrees Sagittarius. Both transiting Rahu and Jupiter cast a trine to each other but natal Jupiter complete a grand trine at 24 degrees Aries. Transiting Jupiter stationed (retrograde) 20 degrees Leo at the time of the win. Rahu was stationing at 16 degrees as well at this time. During the eclipse prior to this event in July, Rahu was stationed at 25 Sagittarius, within a degree of natal Jupiter. Transiting Ketu 16 degrees Gemini was trine natal Mars ruler of the 2nd house of money.

12th h. ☊ 13:56 UBh ♓	1st h. Asc 06:31 Ash ☉ 10:29 Ash ♈	2nd h. ☿ 00:26 Kri ♉	3rd h. ♅ 08:40 Ard ☽ 28:17 Pun ♊
11th h. ♀ 24:38 PBh ♃ 08:25 Sat ♒	Sharon Brown Mon 04-24-1950 04:45:00 Methuen, MA USA		4th h. ♇ 22:36 Asl ♋
10th h. ♑	Timezone: 5 DST: 0 Latitude: 42N43'34 Longitude: 71W11'29 Ayanamsha : -23:09:44 Lahiri		5th h. ♄℞ 19:47 PPh ♂℞ 29:23 UPh ♌
9th h. ♐	8th h. ♏	7th h. ♎	6th h. ☋ 13:56 Has ♆ 22:20 Has ♍

Sharon Brown won 35 million on 10/26/1996

On that day transiting Jupiter was 18 degrees Sagittarius, casting a trine to natal Saturn 19 degrees Leo and completing a grand trine with natal Sun at 10 degrees Aries. Natal Saturn rules the 11th house of great gains.

Transiting Rahu was 14 degrees Virgo conjunct natal Ketu. So the transiting nodes are conjunct the natal nodes. This is called a natal inversion when Rahu conjuncts Ketu and Ketu conjuncts Rahu.

The station of Jupiter (direct) in September was 14 degrees Sagittarius, and Rahu was stationing at 14 degrees in October at the time of the win.

Note transiting Saturn was 7 degrees Pisces conjunct natal Rahu and transiting Ketu.

2nd h. ♓	3rd h. ♂ 18:58 Bha ♈	4th h. ☋ 00:25 Kri ♉	5th h. ♊
1st h. ☉ 05:17 Dha Asc 02:07 Dha ♒	Kathleen McLaughlin Sun 02-17-1957 06:35:00 Boston, MA USA Timezone: 5 DST: 0 Latitude: 42N21'30 Longitude: 71W03'37 Ayanamsha : -23:15:45 Lahiri		6th h. ♅ 10:42 Pus ♋
12th h. ♀ 21:16 Shr ☿ 13:26 Shr ♑			7th h. ♇ 05:57 Mag ♌
11th h. ♐	10th h. ☊ 00:25 Vis ♄ 20:03 Jye ♏	9th h. ♆ 09:16 Swa ♎	8th h. ♃R 06:56 UPh ☽ 14:33 Has ♍

Kathleen McLaughlin won 27 million on 12/13/1991

On that day transiting Jupiter was 20 degrees Leo trine transiting Rahu 16 degrees Sagittarius, natal Mars fills in the point that both trine creating a grand trine 18 degrees Aries. Transiting Rahu was in the 11th house of great gains.

Both Jupiter and Rahu were stationing on these degrees at the time of this lottery win, empowering these points.

4th h.	5th h.	6th h.	7th h.
☽ 23:54 Rev ♃℞ 14:25 UBh ♓	♈	♉	♅ 20:47 Pun ♊
3rd h. ☊ 16:07 Sat ♒	Clifford Turner Sun 10-14-1951 13:00:00 Brookline, MA USA Timezone: 5 DST: 0 Latitude: 42N19'54 Longitude: 71W07'18 Ayanamsha : -23:11:06 Lahiri		8th h. ♇ 27:59 Asl ♋
2nd h. ♑			9th h. ♂ 12:46 Mag ♀ 15:30 PPh ☋ 16:07 PPh ♌
1st h. Asc 24:47 PSh ♐	12th h. ♏	11th h. ♎	10th h. ♄ 14:10 Has ♆ 26:08 Cht ☉ 27:23 Cht ☿ 28:12 Cht ♍

Clifford Turner won 50 million on 03/19/2004.

On that day transiting Jupiter was 18 degrees Leo and Rahu was 17 degrees Aries. Both Rahu and Jupiter trine each other and transiting Jupiter is conjunct natal Ketu, Venus and Mars in the 9th house of luck and fortune. Transiting Ketu is aspecting natal Rahu. Frequently the transiting lunar nodes are aspecting the natal lunar nodes.

Jupiter was stationed (stationary retrograde) in January at 24 Leo, which was trine the Ascendant degree. Rahu was stationed at 17 degrees, the same degree at the time of the win. If you include the Ascendant degree 24 degrees Sagittarius there is a grand trine with transiting Rahu 17 Aries, Transiting Jupiter 18 degrees Leo, and transiting Jupiter is conjunct natal Ketu, Venus and Mars.

5th h.	6th h.	7th h.	8th h.
☉ 24:47 Rev ♓	♇℞ 03:04 Ash ♂ 20:26 Bha ♃ 29:41 Kri ♈	♉	♅ 21:20 Pun ♊
4th h. ☿ 28:40 PBh ♒	Katherine Ippolito Tue 04-07-1953 22:32:00 Everett, MA USA Timezone: 5 DST: 0 Latitude: 42N24'30 Longitude: 71W03'15 Ayanamsha : -23:12:28 Lahiri		9th h. ☋ 16:34 Pus ♀ 27:43 Asl ♋
3rd h. ☊ 16:34 Shr ☽ 06:50 USh ♑			10th h. ♌
2nd h. ♐	1st h. Asc 15:14 Anu ♏	12th h. ♄℞ 01:13 Cht ♎	11th h. ♆ 29:26 Cht ♍

Katherine Ippolito won 2 million on 01/19/1992.

On that day transiting Jupiter was 20 degrees Leo and transiting Rahu was 16 degrees Sagittarius. Both transiting Rahu and Jupiter trine natal Mars at 20 degrees Aries, forming a grand trine in the fire signs. The stations of both Jupiter and Rahu occurred at the same time of the win, so these degrees were also the stationary degrees.

Transiting Rahu was in the 2nd house of money activating the three Artha houses, 2, 6, and 10. Artha houses pertain to material things in life, such as money, possessions, work and career.

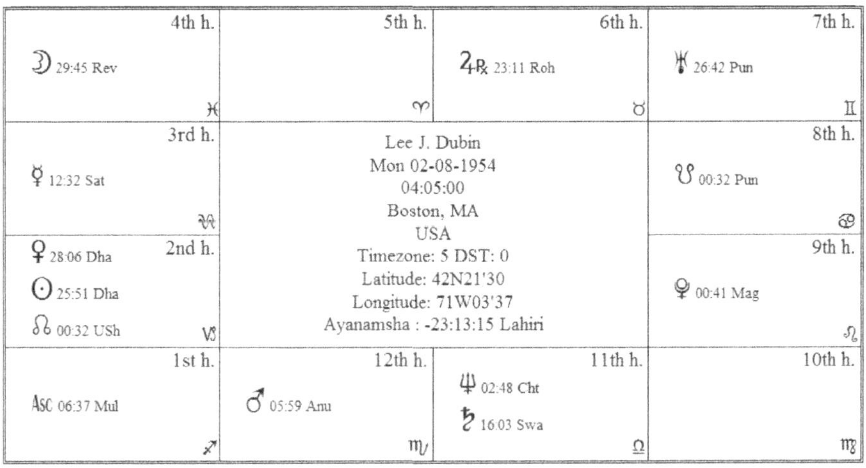

Lee Dubin won 26 million on 06/25/1994.

On that day transiting Jupiter was 11 degrees Libra and transiting Rahu was also in Libra 29 degrees, both conjunct natal Saturn in the 11th house of gains, casting a trine to natal Mercury at 12 degrees Aquarius.

Jupiter was stationed (stationary direct) in June at the time of the win at 11 degrees of Libra.

Transiting Rahu stationed in May at 0 degrees Scorpio casting a trine to natal Ketu. Again the transiting lunar nodes are aspecting the natal nodes.

<table>
<tr><td>7th h.
☉ 06:04 UBh
♓</td><td>8th h.
♀ 20:18 Bha
♈</td><td>9th h.
☋ 17:43 Roh
♉</td><td>10th h.
☽ 09:10 Ard
♊</td></tr>
<tr><td>6th h.
☿ 20:32 PBh
♒</td><td colspan="2" rowspan="2">Robert Abney
Mon 03-19-1956
17:55:00
Boston, MA
USA
Timezone: 5 DST: 0
Latitude: 42N21'30
Longitude: 71W03'37
Ayanamsha : -23:15:01 Lahiri</td><td>11th h.
♅ 05:05 Pus
♃℞ 29:29 Asl
♋</td></tr>
<tr><td>5th h.
♑</td><td>12th h.
♇ 03:22 Mag
♌</td></tr>
<tr><td>4th h.
♂ 19:54 PSh
♐</td><td>3rd h.
♄℞ 09:30 Anu
☊ 17:43 Jye
♏</td><td>2nd h.
♆ 06:34 Cht
♎</td><td>1st h.
Asc 06:51 UPh
♍</td></tr>
</table>

Robert Abney won 1 million on 04/02/2003

On that day transiting Jupiter was 14 degrees Cancer and transiting Ketu was 6 degrees Scorpio casting a trine to each other, they both aspect the natal Sun at 6 degrees Pisces completing a grand trine.

Transiting Ketu is conjunct natal Rahu and transiting Rahu is conjunct natal Ketu and it is aspecting the Ascendant degree at 6 degrees Virgo.

Jupiter was stationed, (stationary direct) in April at the time of the win at 14 degrees of Cancer, It turned stationary retrograde in December 2002 at 24 degrees Cancer very close to the conjunction of natal Jupiter at 29 degrees Cancer in the 11th house of gains.

Note natal Saturn is conjunct natal Rahu and transiting Ketu is conjunct natal Saturn and Rahu as well. Transiting Saturn was at 29 Taurus aspecting natal Jupiter 29 Cancer, and conjunct natal Ketu in the 9th house.

3rd h. ☊ 05:12 UBh ♓	4th h. ♈	5th h. ♉	6th h. ♅ 15:56 Ard ♊
2nd h. ♃℞ 06:38 Dha ♒	Paula Moore Sat 09-16-1950 16:15:00 Lawrence, MA USA Timezone: 5 DST: 1 Latitude: 42N42'25 Longitude: 71W09'49 Ayanamsha : -23:10:07 Lahiri		7th h. ♇ 25:44 Asl ♋
1st h. Asc 01:45 USh ♑			8th h. ♀ 15:12 PPh ♄ 29:36 UPh ♌
12th h. ♐	11th h. ♂ 00:40 Vis ☽ 03:15 Vis ♏	10th h. ♎	9th h. ☉ 00:12 UPh ☿℞ 01:11 UPh ☋ 05:12 UPh ♆ 23:02 Has ♍

Paula Moore won 24 million on 03/17/1997

On that day transiting Jupiter was 18 degrees Capricorn and transiting Rahu was 4 degrees Virgo. They are casting a trine to each other from the earth signs. Transiting Rahu is conjunct natal Ketu in Virgo and transiting Ketu is conjunct natal Rahu in Pisces. Transiting Rahu is in the 9th house of luck and fortune conjunct natal Sun, Mercury and Ketu. Transiting Jupiter is trine this house. Transiting Rahu is trine the Ascendant degree of 1 degree Capricorn.

The station of Jupiter (stationary retrograde) was 23 degrees Sagittarius in May 1996 and the stationary direct was in December, 1996 at 14 degrees Sagittarius. At both stations natal Venus and Saturn are closely trine by transiting Jupiter. Venus and Saturn are in the 8th house of unearned money.

The station of Rahu was at the same time as the win at 4 degrees of Virgo.

Transiting Saturn was 14 Pisces conjunct natal Rahu and transiting Ketu aspecting the 9th natal house planets as well as Sun, Mercury, and Ketu.

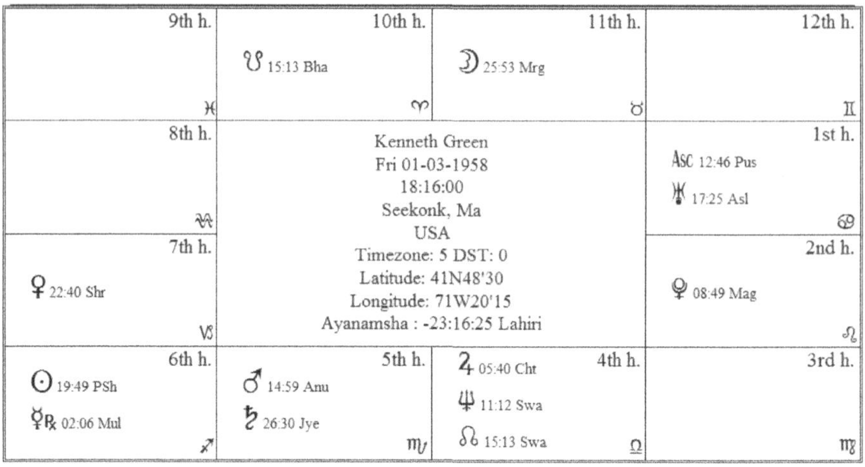

Kenneth Green won 13 million on 12/22/1992

On that day transiting Jupiter was 18 degrees Virgo, and transiting Rahu 27 degrees Scorpio and transiting Ketu 27 Taurus. Transiting Ketu is trine transiting Jupiter and both cast a trine to natal Venus at 22 Capricorn completing the grand trine. Transiting Ketu is conjunct the natal Moon which is also involved in this grand trine, for transiting Ketu, 27 Taurus conjuncts the natal Moon, 25 Taurus and transiting Jupiter, 18 Virgo trines it ,and all are trine natal Venus, 22 Capricorn. The Moon is in the 11th house of gains and natal Venus rules this house.

Rahu is stationary at the time of the win at 27 degrees of Scorpio. It is conjunct natal Saturn, 26 Scorpio in the 5th house of speculation.

Transiting Saturn is 21 degrees Capricorn conjunct natal Venus, which is the natal planet involved in the grand trine of transiting Ketu and transiting Jupiter.

Prior stations were Jupiter (stationary retrograde) in January at 20 degrees of Leo and in April (stationary direct) 10 degrees Leo. These stations were previously transiting the 2nd house aspecting the natal Sun 19 Sagittarius and natal Ketu 15 degrees Aries.

The transiting and natal lunar nodes did not aspect at this time.

Conclusion

There are many variables to consider when analyzing a chart in terms of a sudden rise in fortune and luck. These events are foreseen as the specific karmas of a soul in this lifetime and seem to be activated as to the time of occurrence with the cyclic processes of the transiting planets. There does seem to be specific variables pointing to the trine aspect, transiting Jupiter and Rahu/Ketu and their degrees around stations.

We perceive great gains of money as a lucky and fortunate event but the after effects could be interesting as to the karma these individuals create through their sudden gains of fortune. Is it a blessing or a curse? Here is where freewill comes into play as these individual's decide what they will do with their fortune.

Chapter 10

How to Find the Most Auspicious Hours: Planetary Hours

"The controls of life are structured as forms and nuclear arrangements, in a relation with the motions of the universe."

Louis Pasteur

This is a tool used by the ancients. It is very fundamental and simple to use, but it should be lined up with other factors in your own personal chart to find your lucky times during a day. I have found this technique definitely works.

The planetary hours are based on the day of the week. Each day of the week is named after a planet and each day when the Sun rises the planet that rules that day begins the first hour of the day. Then each hour following proceeds in the same order. The times between sunrise and sunset is divided into 12 equal parts, each is called a Planetary Hour. Likewise the time from sunset to sunrise is also divided into 12 equal parts which are the planetary hours of night.

The beginning hour of each day depends on the planet that rules that day. Then the specified order begins, here is the fixed order that each day follows beginning with the planet that rules that day; Saturn, Jupiter, Mars, Sun, Venus, Mercury and Moon. They appear to be in the order of their apparent motion or speed in their orbits from earth.

For example: on Sunrise on Sunday the initial first hour of the day is the Sun, followed by the next hour ruled by Venus, Mercury, Moon, Saturn, Jupiter, Mars, and so on repeating this in the same order. This continues throughout the night till the following day where it will come back around to the planet at sunrise which will then be the same planetary hour for the planet that rules that day at sunrise. So throughout the day and night at the next sunrise the planet ruling that day would be the Moon which is the day of Monday.

Planetary Rulers for each Day of the Week
Sunday/Sun
Monday/Moon
Tuesday/Mars
Wednesday/Mercury
Thursday/Jupiter
Friday/Venus
Saturday/Saturn

The most important thing to know about the planetary hours is to carefully choose a good planetary hour to begin an event to make sure it will be successful. Jupiter is usually the best planetary hour to begin things you want to succeed or be lucky. Venus is another lucky hour that can produce happiness.

I was on a trip in Reno, Nevada and I knew the hotel had gambling. So before I went I analyzed the chart of my husband, in which I knew he had lucky aspects occurring in his chart. I charted the Jupiter planetary hour and told him to pull the lever of a slot machine at that precise time. I told him it was the Jupiter hour. At that exact time he won $1,200.00. That isn't an amount that will change our lives but it did validate the power of the Jupiter hour, for the rest of the time he didn't win at all.

My first astrology teacher always used the planetary hour system. He told me when ever there was any kind of raffle he made sure he bought his ticket at the Jupiter hour. He used to do this at astrology conferences. He won every time and stood up to announce "See astrology does work".

I know the planetary hours work if you use them in conjunction with other specific favorable transits happening in your own individual chart.

Sun's hour: It is a good hour for dealings with bosses, public officials, or influential people. It is the best time to spend with your father. Overall it is not a good time for others for misunderstandings can occur.

Moon's hour: good time to deal with women, particularly your mother. It is a good time to conceive a baby, perfect time for cooking, nurturing and caring for others.

Mars' hour: Is the hour you may find yourself in an argument, or stopped by the police. It is not good for leaving to go on a trip. It is a good time for surgery or anything that requires sharp precision.

Mercury's hour: Is a great time to take tests or study. It gives focus to all mental pursuits. It is great for all forms of communications such as speaking and writing. It is a good time to leave on a trip.

Jupiter's hour: this is the lucky time and brings expansion and optimism to all affairs. It is also a great time for leaning and study especially spiritual subjects. This is a perfect time to begin trips or long journeys.

Venus' hour: Is a happy time, social events should be planned during this hour. It is a time of love, romance or marriage. Good for purchase of luxury items like a car.

Saturn's hour: Is a time to retreat and be alone. Connecting to others is difficult now. It is a great time to begin a diet or a fast.

Chapter 11

Best Times for Luck and Success

"Aligning with Positive Energy"

"Oh the wonderful knowledge to be found in the star.
Even the smallest things are written there...
if you had but skill to read."

Ben Franklin

There are many who believe we have free will and we can overcome anything with proper will and determination, and others who feel we have karma and everything will happen as pre destined. I think it is a little of both. I feel there is much we must experience for our growth spiritually. How we navigate within these seeming predestined events will determine the outcome. We are born with particular personalities and an emotional nature. These attributes are the makings of our past karmic experiences. As we grow on a spiritual level we are drawn to certain interests. What interests us as a teenager will not fascinate us as a young adult or as a senior citizen. We grow in awareness with each life experience. The patterns in our astrological chart indicate certain experiences throughout our life. Knowing when to make our move in accordance to our astrological chart is so very helpful. Our astrological chart is like a road map to navigate through our life.

There is a time and a place to do certain things for the best results. There is a time to plant certain crops according to the seasons and certainly a time and a place to meet people. But with the advantage of astrology you can pick the days you are best suited to get the results you want.

In terms of financial prosperity there are times to push and move forward with a business and a time to pull back and lay low.

Your mind set is important as well. When the aspects in a chart get difficult we must remember to keep a positive mind, for negativity only breeds more problems. It is important to know challenging aspects are meant to produce breakthroughs and spiritual growth. A positive frame of mind is essential to make the best of these difficult times for these times in our lives are what push us to reach our higher goals.

To choose a time for an event to get the best results is called electional astrology. This is the birth of the event. This creates a birth chart for the event, and as the planets continue to transit through the chart indicates events will continue to emerge through the interaction of the transiting planets to the natal planets. Electional astrology is used for any important event such as choosing dates for a marriage, surgery, opening of a business, changing residence, or going on a trip or vacation.

To find the best timing for certain events the natural benefics must be placed accordingly. In a 24 hour period the ascendant moves through the entire zodiac. The ascendant is the sign that rises on the eastern horizon. It moves 4 degrees every minute, and changes signs every 2 hours. Therefore, it will complete the entire zodiac of 12 signs in a 24 hour period; 2 (Hours) X 12 (Signs) = 24 Hours. The sign on the ascendant determines what signs are on all of the 12 houses, therefore places all the planets in a house depending on what sign each planet is transiting in.

It has been said by the great masters that if you choose a time when the benefics are on the ascendant you cancel any problems that the chart may have. That is if you can time it when either Jupiter or Venus are exactly on the degree rising you will have an extraordinary chart for luck and success for almost any endeavor you may be planning. This means you have around a 4 minute window. It can be a few degrees off but the closer to exact degree the better.

Have you ever noticed when you may be having a winning streak then suddenly your luck changes? Of course you have! This pertains to the planets that may be rising over the current ascendant degree, not the ascendant degree in your own chart, but the ascendant degree that is currently happening. When benefic planets rise over the ascendant degree it can cancel out any negative aspects occurring in the sky. But when malefic planets rise over the ascendant degree it can cause fights, accidents, and problems. This all takes place within a 24 hour period. This is not specific to your own chart therefore, can be used by everyone.

The natural benefics are Jupiter, Venus, and Mercury and the natural malefics are Saturn, Mars, Sun, and Ketu. The Moon will cause extreme fluctuations and Rahu is mainly malefic but in some cases expands and brings things of benefit to you.

Since the entire zodiac of planets pass through the ascendant degree within every 24 hours we can chart when the planets will arrive there. We can plan when Jupiter will be on the ascendant. This may occur at 3:00 AM which is not a time to plan meetings, but you can find the times within the year that it is possible to plan meetings or sign contracts for the best possible outcome when either, Jupiter, Venus or Mercury are rising across the ascendant. This will give you great opportunities.

Currently, Jupiter is in Pisces so the time that the sign Pisces rises across the eastern horizon would be an auspicious time for prosperity. For example; August 19th, 2010 at 9:40 PM in Dallas, Texas, Jupiter would be rising exactly on the ascendant at 8 degrees of Pisces. I simply chose the time that the ascendant degree became the same degree as Jupiter this day. You can find the times within the year that certain signs with benefic planets are rising within each day.

The calculations are not hard to figure out, for any astrological program can do this for you. The point is you can choose the auspicious times to do things in accordance with where the planets are in your time and space. While 9:40 PM is not a convenient time to make plans, there are times within a day within the year that you can make plans when Jupiter will be on the current ascendant. Likewise, you would take note of where the malefic planets are and avoid the times they would rise across the ascendant. Currently, Saturn is opposed Jupiter so it will rise on the ascendant around 10:40 AM, which will be a difficult time for most activities, and to avoid meetings would be wise since malefic Saturn is on the ascendant at this time and date.

If a benefic on the ascendant is not possible then the benefic planets must be in the appropriate houses to benefit the electional chart. If it a marriage chart then the 7th house of marriage is fortified for a happy marriage.

For the purposes of luck and fortune it is very important to choose the time when either Jupiter or Venus is rising on the ascendant. If that time is not possible then the benefics must be placed well in the money houses, 2, 11,5, and 9. The 8th house concerns money from others but it is a very difficult house meaning sometimes you have to go through a death (as in inheritance) or a divorce to come into the money this house offers. So you do not want this house fortified. You must avoid any planets in this house.

Transiting Planets aspecting Your Natal Planets for Your Personal Luck

Since we know what patterns produce wealth in an individual's chart we can strategically find times using the transiting planets to mimic the natal aspects someone has that has won the lottery or who has great wealth through their own doing. This means we must look for the winning times. To find this specific time in our chart one of our own natal planets must be involved in the transiting patterns of luck to bring us wealth. But we must plan and be ready to make our move whether it involves buying a lottery ticket or starting out to find a job or opportunity.

The one thing that was clear with the lottery winners was the trinal (120 degree) aspects of both Jupiter and Rahu or Ketu. Or, also not as powerful but good are the times that Jupiter or Rahu/Ketu sextile (60 degree) a personal point in our own charts.

When a birth chart is endowed with natal trine aspects, a transiting planet will set off these trines which can create a grand trine in the chart. For example, a natal birth chart may have Venus 5 degrees of Leo and Saturn is at 6 degrees Sagittarius. When transiting Jupiter transits 5-6 degrees of Aries this will create a grand trine in this chart. The transit of Jupiter has filled in the missing area that hooks up all 3 planets and produces a time of fortune and luck.

Jupiter is the planet revered for wealth and luck. Chart what sign Jupiter is currently transiting and compare the planets in your own birth chart to see when Jupiter will conjunct or trine any of your own personal planets. Jupiter will trine planets that are of the same element. When transiting Jupiter is in a water sign (Cancer, Scorpio, or Pisces) you must find the planets in your chart that are in water signs. Then the times that Jupiter comes to the exact degree that you have a planet in a water sign means Jupiter will either trine or conjunct your planet. The conjunction is in the same sign.

For example, currently Jupiter is in the sign of Pisces, therefore if you have any planets in the signs of Pisces, Cancer or Scorpio, Jupiter will be in trine aspect or conjunct them. Remember, the planets in the same element are *always* trine one another, fire, earth, air and water. You just need to find the day that this aspect is exact.

Fire signs: Aries, Leo, Sagittarius

Earth signs: Taurus, Virgo, Capricorn

Air signs: Gemini, Libra, Aquarius

Water signs: Cancer, Scorpio, Pisces

Jupiter is currently transiting 8 degrees of Pisces and my natal Venus at 10 degrees Scorpio meaning very soon Jupiter will cast a perfect trine to my natal Venus. On that exact day I am lucky and I should pursue the things that I want to happen in my life. Because Jupiter is traveling retrograde currently it will take a bit longer before it will come to the degree of 10 Pisces. Looking at the transits of Jupiter in a planetary ephemeris (book that has the planet's degrees and movements each year) Jupiter will be 10 degrees of Pisces on Lebruary 13th 2011. This day I should plan events around receiving prosperity. Actually, you can prepare things relating to the culminating day or days before this time to assure you will be ready to receive your wishes and fulfillment.

Chart the signs that Rahu and Ketu are transiting, and find the times they aspect your benefic planets (Venus, Jupiter, and Mercury). You are looking for the trines or conjunctions of these planets. If Rahu or Ketu are trining or conjuncting a planet in your chart, then will always sextile the opposite exact point. For example, if you have planet Mercury at 8 degrees of Libra, and transiting Ketu is at 8 degrees of Gemini it will be trining your planet Mercury. The opposite point of Ketu is Rahu at 8 degrees of Sagittarius this would be sextile (60 degrees) your Mercury. When you can find a time when both transiting Rahu or Ketu and benefic Jupiter trine a point in you chart you are *very* lucky and should make plans to achieve you current goals, because you will be successful.

To find the *most* auspicious time calculate the time that transiting Jupiter will cast a trine to another transiting planet and find the time they both cast a trine to only *one* of your natal planets. The difference here is there are 2 planets transiting trining each other and your natal planet fills the empty point that creates the grand trine. It is hard to find a time when 2 planets exactly trine 1 of your natal planets. But it is sure to happen at some point. When you find these special dates you must make plans for you are at your peak with luck.

For example: Transiting Jupiter is casting a trine to transiting Mercury; transiting Jupiter is 8 Pisces and transiting Mercury is 8 Scorpio, look to see if you have a natal planet in a water sign around 8 degrees. This will create a grand trine with one of your natal planets if you have a planet around 8 degrees Cancer, or a conjunction of a natal planet at 8 degrees of Scorpio or Pisces. This will be your time for amazing luck!

*If you find a day that transiting Rahu trines transiting Jupiter and they both trine a natal planet in your chart then there will be a sextile from Ketu to this natal planet in your chart. This is the set up most of the lottery winners had in their charts. Or transiting Ketu trines transiting Jupiter and they both trine one natal planet in your chart therefore Rahu will sextile this natal planet. This is your lucky day!

This does require Jupiter to be in trine aspect to either Rahu or Ketu, which is not operating all the time but is worth the time to figure out when they are.

Sometimes you can find days where you have the benefic planets in sextile to your natal planets. This means they are 3 signs away from each other but you must chart the exact degree that this takes place. That is the day you will have opportunities and be fortunate. The sextiles are not as powerful as the trines but they do help in achieving your goals. For example, if Jupiter is in Pisces then Taurus is the sign that is 3 signs away from Pisces. You count Pisces, to Aries and then Taurus (3 signs away).

This pattern using the signs means that planets that sextile each other are always this pattern:

Fire sextiles Air

Earth sextiles Water

Air sextiles Fire

Water sextiles Earth

Aries: (Fire) Sextiles: Gemini and Aquarius

Taurus: (Earth) Sextiles: Cancer and Pisces

Gemini: (Air) Sextiles: Leo and Aries

Cancer: (Water) Sextiles: Virgo and Taurus

Leo: (Libra) Sextiles: Libra and Gemini

Virgo: (Earth) Sextiles: Scorpio and Cancer

Libra: (Air) Sextiles: Sagittarius and Leo

Scorpio: (Water) Sextiles: Capricorn and Virgo

Sagittarius: (Libra) Sextiles: Aquarius and Libra

Capricorn: (Earth) Sextiles: Pisces and Scorpio

Aquarius: (Air) Sextiles: Aries and Sagittarius

Pisces: (Water) Sextiles: Taurus and Capricorn

It is easier to count 3 signs away from both sides of the planet. Begin the counting with the sign the planet is in. For example: Venus is 10 degrees of Scorpio (Water), the signs that are sextile to Venus are Capricorn and Virgo (Earth). Therefore, when a benefic transiting planet such as Jupiter is either 10 degrees of Capricorn or Virgo this sextile aspect will offer possibilities for opportunities.

The sextiles usually work best when combined with trines occurring simultaneously. A few sextiles without the trines are very subtle and will not produce events on their own. The most auspicious times in your life will include both these aspects occurring at the same time.

For your own personal wealth look when the transiting planets aspect the money houses or the ruler of the money houses (2, 11, 5, and 9) and you will experience growth and prosperity.

To specifically use all these tools, 1) the planetary hours, 2) the electional chart of the current transiting planets in the heavens in relation to 3) the constant flux of the moving ascendant rising across the eastern horizon, and 4) you own personal natal birth chart for the times to succeed in activities, *then you are equipped with the tools to guide you with conscious awareness and ultimate success.*

Chapter 12

Predicting Your Future Transiting Jupiter, Saturn and Rahu/Ketu

"Astrology is astronomy brought down to earth and applied toward the affairs of man. "

Ralph Waldo Emerson

Your own birth chart is set up with your ascendant which is the beginning of the chart figured from your birth time. Once the signs are set on the houses the planets are placed in the houses. The houses they occupy pertain to the areas of life that will be activated.

The transiting planets are what determine *when* events will occur in your life. The transiting planets are the current movements of the planets in the sky and where they will be in the future in your chart will predict trends for future events.

The 1st house is the new beginning as it all relates to you, for the 1st house is the ascendant. The sign on your ascendant will give you the information to plan your life's events. The ascendant sets up all your planets in the houses. The planets to chart initially, to see the overall effects of events to come in your life, would be the transits of Jupiter Saturn and Rahu/Ketu. These planets are the most important for making any predictions, as noted throughout this book, whether for money, love, health, or happiness. The other transiting planets will be triggers for events but the overall picture will be cast by these specific transiting planets Jupiter, Saturn, and Rahu/ Ketu.

1st House

Jupiter Transits the 1st House

The transit of Jupiter in this house will indicate it is time for new beginnings, indicating it is time to make your move, and start new projects. You feel awakened and want to fill your life with new opportunities. This new cycle will actually take 12 years to complete, for Jupiter takes 12 years to transit through the entire 12 zodiacal signs and your chart. To understand what any Jupiter cycle is going to be about revert your attention back to the last time Jupiter was in a certain house by thinking back exactly 12 years ago, and you can see what occurred then, for it will be similar. Jupiter is about expansion so you feel much more positive and want to expand your horizons during the time Jupiter goes through your 1st house. Jupiter is about renewal and confidence. You will feel energized and optimistic. It is a time your self esteem is booming and you attract all kinds of new opportunities into your life. Jupiter represents freedom and you will feel free to begin new projects you previously felt impossible to begin due to previous circumstances and conditions.

Saturn transits the 1st House

The transit of Saturn can cause setbacks for you may be over loaded with heavy responsibilities. Saturn can also indicate that you will have more work than you planned, and you will experience exhaustion and tiredness. Saturn in the 1st house is often about responsibilities that weigh heavy on you. Saturn will remain in a sign for about 2 and a half years, therefore it takes Saturn around 30 years to cycle through the entire zodiac, looking back about that time of 30 years ago can give clues as to what it means for Saturn to be in your 1st house.

Jupiter and Saturn are quit opposite in their effects. One is about expansion and the other about contraction. One good thing about Saturn in the 1st house you usually lose weight but with expansive Jupiter in the 1st house you may put on weight for you are happy and active and may attend more events.

Rahu and Ketu transits the 1st and 7th Houses

The transit of Rahu and Ketu across the ascendant or your 1st house is always eventful for you must realize that where the nodes of the Moon are is where the eclipses are occurring in your chart. This will be the place in your life you experience the most change. As the ascendant is you, this means you will be changing dramatically during this one and a half year period.

The nodal axis of the Moon means Rahu or Ketu will be affecting two opposing houses simultaneously. When one is in the 1st house, the 7th house automatically is a place of tension. The 1st and 7th houses pertain to relationships, meaning your marriage or significant other will come under the tensions of these eclipses occurring in both your 1st and 7th house. The eclipses occur 2 times a year, each six months apart. One eclipse will be with Rahu and the next one with Ketu triggering both opposing houses. During these times relationships will be tested to the most extreme degree and anything that has been repressed will most certainly surface. This is our opportunity to grow through ourselves and our relationships. If the relationship is not on good terms this would definitely cause a break up, but most relationships that are solid will go through a testing period that will strengthen the bond through growth together.

2nd House

Jupiter transits the 2nd House

This is the house of money, especially the money we earn ourselves. It also pertains to what we value, but as seen throughout this book this is the most important house dealing with our money and finances. As Jupiter transits through this house you can generally count on expansion and gains in this area of your life. Jupiter in this house gives you opportunities to gain more income and expand your business portfolio. This would be a time you can take the risks that could cause you to double your financial means. It does matter what sign Jupiter is on the second house for some signs Jupiter is more prosperous, particularly Cancer and Pisces. To have Cancer on the 2nd house means you must have Gemini as the ascendant, and an Aquarius ascendant has Pisces on the 2nd house. These two signs on the ascendant produce the best results when Jupiter is in Cancer or Pisces. While Sagittarius ascendant has Capricorn on the 2nd house cusp, Jupiter in Capricorn is weaker due to its debilitation in this sign. Jupiter in the 2nd house in Capricorn will give some good results financially because of the house, but limited due to the sign placement.

Saturn transits the 2nd House

Saturn transiting your 2nd house will cause you some delays and restraints from receiving the money that is rightfully yours. Many times Saturn will give money as it transits through the 2nd house but it is allocated to you in a certain way that limits you from doing the things you could do without this restriction. This would *not* be a time to overextend yourself for you will have regrets later. This is a time to conserve your money and work harder to acquire more, for then you will be free do anything you wish later when Saturn is finished transiting this house. Sometimes Saturn here can pertain to legacies and inheritances but with the restraints and rules.

Rahu and Ketu Transits the 2nd and 8th Houses

Rahu and Ketu transiting through the 2nd and 8th house pertain exclusively to money. This can be a time of gains and losses during this transit. It could be relative to how you acquire your money. You will be looking at your financial situation as it deals with inheritances as well as money received in a marriage or divorce. Whatever your predicament financially the nodes across these houses will cause disruption. It will produce extremes, so if you are in an expansive time in your life, there will be a dramatic shift conversely, if you have been struggling you could have an unexpected opportunity. Expect the unexpected with money at this time. It isn't wise to take risks during this time.

3rd House

Jupiter Transits the 3rd House

Jupiter in the 3rd house will expand you ability to reach many people with your ideas and plans. You are in a great place to learn and grow with your communicative skills. This is a time of travel for work and pleasure, but most significantly you will learn new exciting information to expand your level or understanding or your expertise. Creativity is at a peak, and new associations with interesting people open doors. Your curiosity creates vision into areas you have never dreamed possible. This is a time to expand your knowledge, take classes and learn from others by observing. Taking many short trips will build your business.

Advertising or some kind of promotion will spread your word or information fast. Be open to opportunities with television, internet or any form of mass communications.

Saturn Transits in the 3rd House

Saturn in the 3rd house gives you the discipline to persevere through the hardest of lessons or classes you thought were impossible. You may feel stifled with your position; therefore you branch out though learning new material to advance yourself. Traveling is curtailed, for there are things that must get done in your current place or location. Saturn here gives discipline, perseverance and determination. You will accomplish your goals for you will not give up, even though you have to work much harder.

Rahu and Ketu transits the 3rd and 9th Houses

Rahu and Ketu in the 3rd and 9th house will promote more travel either by air or on the road. You will have the opportunities to jet out to new places to quench your curious mind. This is a time you will develop your communication skills for you are learning just how important it is to connect through people. Acquiring more connections will promote your business in the future. Unusual subjects seem to inspire and open your mind. There is a definite change in your attitude and your involvement with new people. A quest for higher knowledge keeps you interested in your approach to people and this will change the direction of your life. You will be signing more contracts for business during this period. Business will come from mass communications such as the internet, television, or radio. Be open to new possibilities and new dreams.

4th House

Jupiter transits the 4th House

Jupiter in this house will cause you to think in terms of security. You may want to expand your assets through gains in real estate, or you may just want to change your residence. A desire for a new home with more room or land consumes your mind. Adding on to your current home or to change the look and feel is your main focus.

The 4th house rules all vehicles as well as property therefore you may buy a new car, boat or airplane. It is time that you expand your security through setting up a more secure financial plan for your future. Invest in insurance on your home as well as yourself. You may begin to work out of your home or begin side business. Actually, the 4th house is the house of happiness and Jupiter here produces a sense of well being and contentment. Family matters bring happiness, better relations and connections that will bless your family. Many family celebrations in your home with your family bring fun and contentment.

Saturn transits the 4th House

Saturn in the 4th house will produce much fear about your sense of security. You will want to make sure you do have insurance on your home because now is the time you may really need it. This is a time you will conserve your time and energy for you are fearful for many reasons, realize some of these fears are unfounded.

Since this is the house of happiness Saturn here causes you to be unhappy or discontent with your family. There may be losses with in the family with aging parents, aunts and uncles. Many things in the home tend to break and cause problems. This can also involve problems with cars breaking down so try to keep things serviced and insured. Issues and memories with the past will resurface, so be prepared to heal and grow. Saturn teaches us our most important lessons and what is really important in your life.

Rahu and Ketu transits the 4th and 10th Houses

Rahu and Ketu in the 4th and 10th house will manifest many changes in our home life. People will move in and out of our home. You may sell or purchase a home. There is a deep sense of a lack of security. Your career can determine where you must live during this time. You will not be spending as much time at home. You can have a job opportunity or loss that can move you to a different location. There may be much more expenditure on your home or your car. This is the time you feel less secure about your self worth as well as what you own. Be careful not to overextend yourself with house payments or new items you do not need.

The heart and soul of your life is under fire, and you will feel pressure to change your place in life, where you live and work, but be calm and don't make any dramatic changes during this time because they will not last.

5th House

Jupiter transits the 5th House

This is the house of talent and intelligence which can be very exciting during the time that Jupiter transits this house. You will be full of new ideas to expand your life and business. This is the house of entertainment, opening the door to new places and people. Sporting events, theater and movies move you out of your complacency. You will meet new and interesting people who are on your wave length, who will want to participate in your new ventures. Be alert to new ideas that seem innovative because they are the cutting edge ideas that can make a fortune. This is the house of speculating and you will be moved to experiment with new ways to invest and multiply your finances and bank account. This house can also have a connection to actors, film, or entertainers so be open to where these opportunities take you.

You will be sought out for your advice during this time for you are put into the position of an advisor. Your knowledge and expertise is valuable.

Children in some way can bring you blessings during this time, you may be blessed with a new birth, or your children can achieve awards with great accomplishments.

Saturn transits the 5th House

Saturn transiting the 5th house will bring new responsibilities concerning many important areas you consider meaningful. Children can be a source of responsibility weighting down your life. The kids may now need college or a car. There may be a lot more money spent on your children.

This is a time you will be more concerned with the purpose and meaning in your life, analyzing and contemplating life from a deeper perspective. It is not the time to consider risky investments or investing heavily in the stock market. You are feeling more alone and isolated from people with not much interest to make friends or socialize with others.

Rahu and Ketu transits the 5th and 11th Houses

Rahu and Ketu in the 5th and 11th house cause obsessions and compulsive behaviors you can't seem to control. This is a time of obsessing over ideas and plans. You find yourself thinking of something and cannot get it out of your head. You seem to go over and over different experiences in your past. This is a time when you may come up with extraordinary ideas that can make you rich but be careful for there is a fine line with genius and craziness. You will be intrigued by new ideas that can transform your life in a huge way. The sky is the limit.

Unusual friends and acquaintances will steer you in different directions. Don't let them persuade you into doing things you are not sure about.

Children receive great accomplishments or consume all your free time. No matter what, their accomplishments or problems will overextend you and your time and make you wonder if it is worth it. Make sure you know where they are and who their friends are during this time.

6th House

Jupiter transits the 6th House

This is the house of work, so Jupiter here will produce a great deal of work and much energy exerted in the work place. This will also represent the people you work with whether they are coworkers or employees. This means you will feel supported by your work force. This is a great time to apply for a job or hire new employees. You will acquire the best team and supporters you can find during this time. Interest in heath and diet promotes good habits that motivate you to achieve your goals and start new projects. Prosperity and financial rewards will encourage you to do and achieve more.

Saturn transits the 6th House

Saturn in the 6th house can give more discipline to achieve your goals but you will feel the sense of a heavy responsibility to overcompensate causing you to feel over worked and not appreciated. You may have run ins with your superiors or your business partners. You are doing most of the work and feeling unsupported, tired and exhausted with no end in sight. If you have employees they may quit when you need them the most. Do take care of your health because you can get risk getting sick easier with Saturn here.

Rahu and Ketu transits the 6th and 12th Houses

Rahu and Ketu here can cause great stress to your physical body. A possible health scare can motivate you into changing your habits, which will promote better health in the long run. Those you work with cannot be depended on or trusted, be aware. Generally, if you have employees they seem to quit on you at the most stressful times. This is an opportunity to change your bad habits and change your life.

7th House

Jupiter transits the 7th House

This is the house of relationships that have contractual agreements or have a certain amount of expectation involved. This can represent your marriage partner, a love relationship that is exclusive or a business partnership. When Jupiter transits this house it can bring a new partnership of a lasting value. This partnership makes you feel complete. This is a time that you can expand a business, for you will have the support you need whether it is financial or talent driven. Love and respect are given and returned.

Saturn transits the 7th House

Saturn through the 7th house can cause break ups for it is a time when you will feel a burden or heavy responsibility to keep the relationship intact. The results of enduring this difficult time will be well worth anything you have imagined. It is time to grow through relationships, because if it is a relationship that is worth having you will create a much deeper bond through enduring this time together. Sometimes it can represent problems your partner is experiencing through their lives and you are their supporter and anchor. Saturn means you have to work on your relationship in order for it to grow. This can mean a business partner will need more help during this time. Saturn awakens us to reality, revealing the truth of your relationships. This gives you the information you need to make the right choice.

Rahu or Ketu here have been discussed as they transit through the 1st house. You will definitely have a microscope over your relationships.

8th House

Jupiter transits the 8th House

This is the house of money you own jointly with others, or money you receive through others. It is the house of inheritances, insurance policies, and money from marriage either through joint property or money received through divorce. It pertains to money received that you yourself have not actually earned. Jupiter transiting this house will give in all these areas mentioned. You will receive money through legacies or inheritances. You will have more experiences dealing with death and the other side. Your finances and your bank account will increase. There may be more psychic experiences that keep you in touch with your intuition. The 8th house also represents power mostly through money and will give a certain confidence in this area. Investors are more likely to appear during this time.

Saturn transits the 8th House

Saturn in the 8th house can withhold money that is due to you from others. A divorce settlement will be disappointing, or the amount due to you through inheritances. It has to do with deep lessons concerning money in your lifetime. It can hold up money you need for business. After the wait you may change your mind. If you can learn the deep seated lessons here this will mark a time when you will be very successful once Saturn transits out of this house. Saturn here can transform how you feel about money.

9th House

Jupiter transits the 9th House

Jupiter in the 9th house promotes prosperity and luck. You will be traveling more to spread inspiration and information. Your zeal and optimism is contagious and you know you have a great deal to give to the world. This can be a time you get involved in helping others being a philanthropist. Marketing during this time may involve publications or speaking engagements. Spiritual information that gives your life purpose and meaning opens new possibilities and an inner confidence that leads to success. If you have children of child bearing ages you may be surprised with the news of a new grandchild.

Saturn transits the 9th House

Saturn here can make you a bit cynical so watch your approach to things. At the same time Saturn can make you more realistic. You know what you want because you have realized through difficult experiences what you don't want. Saturn teaches the truth and these facts make your life direction crystal clear. Searching for answers that give your life purpose manifest in everyday occurrences, for this is a time reality sets in. You will be cutting back on any unnecessary or frivolous things in your life. The truth will set you free.

10th House

Jupiter transits the 10th House

The 10th house is the house of your career and anything that pertains to it, particularly your boss or superiors. It can also indicate the government and leaders. Jupiter in this position can lead to career advancement and recognition you receive through your work. This is the house of honors and recognition meaning Jupiter's transit through this house will open possibilities for promotion and advancement. If you own your own business then this will be a very prosperous and expansive time for your business. The 10th house mainly has to do with your social standing in this world. This is the house of fame or recognition in your field of experience.

Saturn transits the 10th House

Saturn in the 10th house can actually help promote your business through all the hard efforts you have put into your work. But Saturn can also mean it is time to restrict and slow down any expansion during this time. It means it is time to pull back and stream line your business possibly because the economy is not conducive to expansion. Saturn is revered as the planet of your just rewards, so according to your efforts you will be rewarded through the transit of Saturn in the 10th house. You could have a boss that is very hard on you, or you may even experience the loss of your boss, being transferred, fired or maybe even through illness. This can also represent takeovers or buy outs of the company you work for.

11th House

Jupiter transits the 11th House

This is the house of great gains, meaning large sums of money you are able to acquire. The 2nd house is also the house of money. Planets in association to the 11th and 2nd houses are the most wealth producing combinations. This is actually the 2nd house from the 10th house meaning it is the house that produces wealth through our career. It represents money that comes in large lump sum amounts. This can pertain to real estate deals, selling a business or any bonuses. When Jupiter transits this house we can usually understand where this money will come for you. It is the result of hard effort and talent you have put forth. Wealth and money can also manifest out of deals you have made with associates and friends. This is the house of important and powerful people and many will assist you during this time. You will be unusually social during this time, with many parties and social events, for you will meet influential people during this time.

Saturn transits the 11th House

Saturn in the 11th house usually will clear out all the unnecessary relationships you may call your friends. The truth and reality about who people really are will surface. This is a time of weeding through the friendships. It seems many people disappoint and drain you of all your energy. You may feel you do not have many friends during this time. It is a natural cleansing for new friends will appear after Saturn has finished transiting this house. The 11th house has been called the house of our ultimate desires and Saturn here will finalize things based on their importance in your life. You may feel a bit disappointed over your achievements, but in reality it is just clearing out all the cob webs for you are in the midst of a transformation and your desires are actually changing. There is a realization of more meaningful goals and aspirations inspiring your life.

12th House

Jupiter transits the 12th House

This is the last and final house of your chart, therefore these transits pertain to endings. It is the house of escape and retreat. And many times relates to foreigners and foreign countries. It actually deals with the last horizons. When Jupiter transits this house you will find it is time to bring things to an end. This is the house of retirement. This may be the ending of a career. This is the house of closure and finalization.

Many times it relates to the past and uncovering issues and problems that held us back, for this is a time of deep self discovery. You will have many unresolved issues surface for healing now. It is definitely not the time to begin a new business, but is time to close one out.

This can be a joyful time of retirement and sending off on well deserved vacations and mysterious journeys abroad. Sometimes it can represent businesses associated with trade and foreign counties. It is a time to prepare for a brand new beginning that is about to occur once Jupiter begins its journey into the 1st house starting new beginnings in a life.

Saturn transits the 12th House

Saturn in the 12th house is usually a time of endings in all areas of life. This is usually not a pleasant experience because there are so many things that surface and must be addressed. It can deal with the demise of your parents and bring final closure to your past. Experiences and events of the past can surface shame and regret. Saturn is reality and when it transits the house of our own undoing it can surface old hurts or pain we have buried so long ago. This can be a transformational time and necessary for our spiritual development. We do come to terms with the dark aspects of our selves, but a healing will conquer many psychological problems, clearing the air for a new and successful life.

Saturn has to be somewhere transiting in a chart, since Saturn is the reality planet it opens our eyes to what we need to know for our highest growth on a mental, emotional and spiritual level. Saturn is our teacher and gives our most important lessons concerning ourselves. All our experiences in life, whether they are about money, love, happiness or security revolve around our spiritual growth. We are all here to understand who we are, and that we are all connected through the Divinity of the Oneness. And through our relationship with money, wealth, love and happiness we will arrive at the same destination.

****

Money has taught me more about myself than any other thing in this world. Saturn will help guide us to our true home, stripping us of the illusion, revealing the truth. Everything is transitory and ephemeral in this world therefore not secure. Realize that we are all the same and the amount of money we possess during our stay here can direct certain behaviors, this is why money has the bad connotations we have been led to believe. Money is energy and can promote comfort and freedom for all. Money is not to be hoarded, used to control others, give power or prestige. All these activities are motivated by fear and lack. It is to be shared and give knowledge for growth on all levels, physical, emotional and spiritual. This awareness can bring joy and happiness to those who realize there is no lack of wealth unless you believe it in your mind.

May Money Guide you to Understanding your Truth!

The Three Wise Men were Astrologers. Some believe that they heard that the Christ child would be born at the time of a conjunction of planets - two planets appearing in the same place in the sky at the same time - that was to signal the arrival of a new age. The two planets involved in this conjunction were ***Jupiter and Saturn****. Both planets were bright, but this wasn't something that the average eye could notice. Even though they were trained astrologers this took The Three Wise Men some time to find Jesus in Bethlehem.*

Joni Patry

Joni has attained the highest level of achievement in her field of Vedic astrology and is revered as one of the most recognized teachers and Vedic astrologers in America. Her writings are intended to inspire others to become aware of our true nature and to understand why we are here on this earth. We are all meant to inspire and teach the truth.

She has been the online Vedic Instructor for the Online College of Astrology, a western astrological certification program. Her course,

Introduction to Vedic Astrology, is accredited by major astrological organizations. She has also taught for the American College of Vedic astrology online program and is a faculty member for ACVA (American Council of Vedic Astrology). She served as the executive secretary for CVA (Council of Vedic Astrology) where she published and distributed the International CVA Journal.

Joni has organized the ACVA International Symposiums held in Hawaii, and organized the first national conference of its kind, "Eastern Astrology for Western Minds" to teach Vedic Astrology to Western astrologers. With an extensive background in Western astrology, Joni dedicates herself to bridging the gap in East/West disciplines by teaching Western astrologers how to incorporate Eastern techniques into their practice.

She has lectured at national and international conferences such as BAVA (British Association of Vedic Astrology), ISAR (International Society for Astrological Research), UAC (United Astrology Conference), ACVA (International Symposiums for the American Council of Vedic Astrology), Eastern Astrology for Western Minds Conference and the Blast. She is the keynote speaker for national and international conferences, and has been on national television and radio programs as an authority on both Western and Vedic astrology. Her clientele includes the who's who of America and Hollywood celebrities.

Her book Eastern *Astrology for Western Minds: A compilation of Neo-Vedic Astrology* is a complete manual to learn Vedic astrology. Joni's book A waken to the Power within You is written to inspire us to seek our true reality. Her book Answers gives the power to know that we have our own connection to the Divine and that we have our own answers within ourselves.

List of published books:

1. Eastern Astrology for Western Minds
2. Finding Money, Luck, and Good Fortune Using Astrology
3. Astrology – The Divine Order of the Universe: Houses, Numbers, Signs and Planets
4. You Are a Star Discover Who You Are (Children's book)
5. Astrologer's Secrets My Best Tools and Techniques
6. Rahu and Ketu: Our Karmic Destiny Revealed Through Eclipses
7. Secrets of Prediction: World and Personal Cycles using Vedic Astrology
8. Uranus: Radical Changes and Awakenings: A NEO-VEDIC Approach
9. Pluto: Control, Power, Surrender and Rebirth: A NEO-VEDIC Approach
10. Neptune Secrets, Illusions and Scandals: A Neo-Vedic Approach
11. Moon Mind and Consciousness
12. Awaken to the Power within You

Bibliography

Chapter 1: Astrology and Money

Yogananda, Paramahansa. The Autobiography of a Yogi, Self Realization Fellowship, Los Angeles, CA 1971

Chapter 2: The Basics of Astrology (Vedic)

Patry, Joni. Eastern Astrology for Western Minds, Galactic Center, Dallas, TX, 2004

Chapter 3: How to Predict World Events with Astrology

Patry, Joni. Eastern Astrology for Western Minds, Galactic Center, Dallas, TX, 2004 Brady Bernadette. The Eagle and the Lark, Samuel Weiser, USA 1999

Chapter 4: Global Planetary Cycles

Patry, Joni. Eastern Astrology for Western Minds, Galactic Center, Dallas, TX, 2004

Chapter 5: Past Astrological Timelines Reveal the Future

Jensen, Richard J. "The Causes and Cures of Unemployment in the Great Depression," *Journal of Interdisciplinary History* 19 (1989)

Kennedy, David. *Freedom from Fear: The American People in Depression and War, 1929-1945* (1999), wide-ranging survey by leading scholar; online edition

McCraw, Thomas K. *American Business, 1920-2000: How It Worked.* 2000

Chapter 6: Is there Money in my Chart?

Birth data and biographies obtained from AstroData Bank Program by Lois Rodden

Chapter 7 How to Determine Career or Life Purpose

Patry, Joni. Classes and CDs from the Galactic Center, Dallas, TX, 2003

Birth data and biographies obtained from AstroData Bank Program by Lois Rodden

Chapter 8: How to use Astrology for the Stock Market

Meridian, Bill. Planetary Stock Trading, Cycles Research, 2000

Chapter 9 How to Predict a Sudden Rise in Life

Patry, Joni. Classes, Articles from Galactic Center website, Dallas, TX 2010
Birth data and biographies obtained from AstroData Bank Program by Lois Rodden

Chapter 10 How to Find Most Auspicious Hours

Patry, Joni. Classes and articles Galactic Center Website, Dallas, TX 2009

Chapter 11: Best Times for Luck and Success

Wilhelm, Ernst. Classical Muhurta, Kala Occult Publishers, 2003

Chapter 12: Predicting Your Future

Patry, Joni. Classes, Articles from Galactic Center website, Dallas, TX 2008
All Astrological data is from AstroData Bank by Lois Rodden Charts calculated by Parashara's Light by Geo vision Software

CONTACT

www.galacticcenter.org
www.universityofvedicastrology.com
YouTube: Joni Patry
Instagram @jonipatry